COLLECTIVE OWNERSHIP

COLLECTIVE OWNERSHIP

OTHERWISE THAN BY CORPORATIONS
OR BY MEANS OF THE TRUST

(BEING THE YORKE PRIZE ESSAY FOR THE YEAR 1905)

BY

C. T. CARR, M.A., LL.M.,

Late Scholar of Trinity College, Cambridge;
Of the Inner Temple and Western Circuit, barrister-at-law.

CAMBRIDGE :

at the University Press

1907

CAMBRIDGE
UNIVERSITY PRESS

University Printing House, Cambridge CB2 8BS, United Kingdom

Published in the United States of America by Cambridge University Press, New York

Cambridge University Press is part of the University of Cambridge.

It furthers the University's mission by disseminating knowledge in the pursuit of education, learning and research at the highest international levels of excellence.

www.cambridge.org
Information on this title: www.cambridge.org/9781107645431

First published 1907
First paperback edition 2014

A catalogue record for this publication is available from the British Library

ISBN 978-1-107-64543-1 Paperback

PREFACE.

THE subject of the following pages is *Collective Ownership otherwise than by Corporations or by means of the Trust.* Of such Collective Ownership it is usual to distinguish four forms: (i) Tenancy by Entireties, (ii) Co-parcenary, (iii) Joint Tenancy, and (iv) Tenancy in Common. In each case it will be seen that the writings of Littleton and Coke remain the foundation of our law. Examples of these four classes of co-owners, compared with examples of sole or corporate ownership, are rare and perhaps are becoming rarer, unless partnership is to be considered an example of either joint tenancy or tenancy in common. Since partners appear to differ materially from other co-owners, partnership is separately treated in Chapter VI.

The rights and remedies of co-owners *inter se* are vague, although Chancery has modified the "barbarous and antiquated" doctrines of the common law. According to Littleton, where there are co-owners of a horse, an ox or a cow, "if the one takes the whole to himselfe out of the possession of the other, the other hath no other remedy but to take this from him who hath done to him the wrong...when he can see his time." The common law was slow to interfere: it hesitated to apply the doctrines of agency or trusteeship: it declined the impossible task of insisting that co-owners should observe equality of use and enjoyment. While statutory and equitable remedies were on the way, more might have been done for an aggrieved co-owner, had he not for the most part already possessed some means of dissolving the co-ownership. This simple remedy was too final for the purposes of partnership, since partners contemplate continuity. Consequently the course and convenience of trade demanded that special rules be made in the case of partnership property or of ships owned in common[1].

A final chapter is added upon *Communities as Owners*. This subject can scarcely be severed from that of corporate ownership which was treated in a previous essay. It seemed, however, a necessary part of a discussion of Collective Ownership, especially since increasing attention is now being attracted to the ownership of land by communities both in the past and in the future.

[1] A valuable note in Lindley's *Partnership* (pp. 32–8) contains the best and fullest statement of the law.

C. T. C.

October 1907

CONTENTS.

PAGE

PREFACE v

LIST OF CASES CITED ix

CHAPTER I.
INTRODUCTION 1

CHAPTER II.
MAN AND WIFE 4

CHAPTER III.
CO-HEIRS 18

CHAPTER IV.
JOINT TENANTS 30

CHAPTER V.
TENANTS IN COMMON 49

CHAPTER VI.
PARTNERS 59

CHAPTER VII.
RIGHTS AND REMEDIES OF CO-OWNERS *INTER SE* . 69

CHAPTER VIII.
COMMUNITIES AS OWNERS 98

INDEX 111

LIST OF CASES CITED.

PAGES

Abergavenny, Case of Lord 38
Alexander v. Simms 62, 87
Amies v. Skillern 33
Apollo, The 85
Archdeacon Carowe's Case 27
Armstrong v. Armstrong 43
Arthur v. Lamb 76
Aston v. Smallman 35
Atcheson v. Atcheson... ... ... 12, 14
Att.-Gen. v. Bacchus 12, 14
Att.-Gen. v. Hamilton 47
Aveling v. Knipe 40

Back v. Andrews 11, 14
Bailey v. Hobson 76
Baker, In re, Pursey v. Holloway 25
Ballard v. Ballard 53
Balmain v. Shore 63
Barker v. Giles... 39
Barnardiston v. Chapman 86, 94
Barton's Will, In re 43
Barton v. Williams 61, 94
Beaumont Peerage Case 23
Bedford, Duke of, v. Ellis 35
Bedford v. Brutton 66
Bence v. Gilpin 34, 45
Bennett v. Holbeach 31
Bentley v. Bates 77, 83
Berens v. Fellows 25
Bevan v. Webb 72
Bishop of Norwich's Case 52
Biss, In re, Biss v. Biss 70, 83
Blaiberg and Abrahams, In re 41
Bleech v. Balleras 65
Bolton v. Salmon 56

a 3

PAGES

Booreman's Case 103
Booth v. Parks... 61
Borwell v. Abey, Doe dem. 50
Bosanquet v. Wray 66
Boson v. Sandford 86
Bracebridge v. Cook 43
Bradshaw v. Toulmin... 36
Brigge v. Brigge 47
Brightwaltham, Case of Village of... 104
Broadbent v. Ledward 35
Brogden, In re... 31
Broughton v. Randall 36, 38
Brown v. Dale 60
Brown v. Hedges 91
Brown v. Raindle 36, 38, 43
Brown v. Tapscott 65
Bryan, In re, Godfrey v. Bryan 12
Buck, In re, Bruty v. Mackey 103
Buckhurst, Case of Lord 72
Buckley v. Barber 60, 61
Burnaby v. Equitable Reversionary Interest Society 44
Burroughs v. McCreight 24
Butler's Trusts, In re, Hughes v. Anderson 43

Cahill v. Cahill 6
Caldwell v. Fellowes 44
Caledonian Coal Co. v. Seaham Colliery Co. 80, 95
Calmady v. Calmady 47
Calvert v. Adams 74
Carowe, Case of Archdeacon 27
Carritt v. Real and Personal Advance Co. 41
Carter v. Horne 80
Case de Tanistry, Le... 21
Cavander v. Bulteel 83
Chamberlain of London's Case 60
Chamier v. Tyrell 12, 17, 33
Chamier v. Willett 56
Chedington, Case of Rector of 11, 42
Chester, Case of Earldom of 27, 28
Chester v. Willan 45
Childs v. Westcot 45
Cisn' v. Ashstead 52
Clegg v. Clegg 80
Clifford's Inn Case 103
Coffee v. Brian 65
Collector of Customs, R. v. 60
Colling's Settled Estates, In re 84

PAGES

Cook's Mortgage, In re, Lawledge v. Tyndale 81
Cook v. Cook 39
Cooper v. Belsey 84
Cooper v. France 23
Coryton v. Lithebye 54, 55
Cowper v. Fletcher 42, 45
Cox v. Hickman 63
Crawshay v. Collins 60
Cray v. Willis 39
Cresswell v. Hedges 73
Crosthwaite v. Dixon, Doe dem. 25
Cubitt v. Porter 73
Cullen v. Knowles and Birks 35
Cunnack v. Edwards 103
Cutting v. Derby 55

Dale v. Hamilton 60
David and Matthews, In re 60, 61
Davis v. Davis 62, 64
Davis v. Johnston 86
Dean v. Wade 26
Decharmis v. Horwood 24
Delamore v. Thwing 24, 27
Dent v. Turpin 58, 90
De Tastet v. Shaw 66
Devaynes v. Noble, Sleech's Case 59
Dias v. de Liviera 14, 15
Dixon, In re, Byram v. Tull 16
Doddington v. Hallet 87
Doe dem. Borwell v. Abey 50
Doe dem. Crosthwaite v. Dixon 25
Doe dem. Gill v. Pearson 34
Doe v. Prosser 73
Drummer v. Pitcher 38
Drury v. Drury 26
Duchy of Lancaster, Case of 106
Duke of Bedford v. Ellis 35
Dunnicliff and Bagley v. Mallet 57
Durham Railway Co. v. Wawn 76
Duvergier v. Fellows 108

Earl of Sussex v. Temple 32, 33
Earldom of Chester, Case of 27, 28
Earle v. Kingscote 15
Edwards v. Champion 44
Elizabeth and Jane, The 85
Elliot v. Brown 60

PAGES

Elwin *v.* Moor ...   60

Eustace *v.* Scawen   45

Ex parte Harrison   87

Ex parte Parke, *In re* Potter   57

Ex parte Young   87

Farrar *v.* Bestwick   94

Featherstonhaugh *v.* Fenwick   83

Fells *v.* Read ...   103

Fennings *v.* Lord Grenville ...   92, 95

Field *v.* Craig ...   96

Finnegan *v.* Noerenberg   109

Fisher's Will, *In re* Trustees of   30

Fleming *v.* Fleming ...   40

Foley *v.* Addenbrooke...   35

Forrest *v.* Whiteway ...   36

Foster *v.* Allanson   65

Foster *v.* Crabb   72

Freestone *v.* Parratt ...   11

French *v.* Styring   65, 96

Frewen *v.* Relfe   43

Fromont *v.* Coupland...   63

Gale *v.* Gale ...   44

Garrick *v.* Taylor   40

Gill *v.* Pearson, Doe dem.   34

Goodtitle *v.* Tombs   73

Goodwyn *v.* Spray   76

Gordon *v.* Whieldon ...   15

Gosling *v.* Gosling   38

Graves *v.* Sawcer   86

Green d. Crew *v.* King   11, 13

Green *v.* Briggs   62, 87, 97

Green's Settlement, *In re*   36

Greenwood's Trusts, *In re*   36

Gregory *v.* Hartnall ...   66

Griffies *v.* Griffies   77

Grute *v.* Locroft   11, 42

Gue, *In re*, Smith *v.* Gue   16

Gully *v.* Bishop of Exeter   27

Haddelsey *v.* Adams ...   50

Hakebeche *v.* Hakebeche   71

Hales *v.* Petit ...   32

Hales *v.* Ridley   33

Hall *v.* Huffam   60

Haly *v.* Goodson   87

PAGES

Hambledon *v.* Hambledon 73
Hamilton *v.* Denny 82
Hammond *v.* Douglas 60
Hamond *v.* Jethro 60
Hancock *v.* Bewley 90
Hargrave *v.* Hargrave... 75
Harman and Uxbridge and Rickmansworth Railway Co., *In re* 41
Harper *v.* Godsell 57, 94, 95
Harrison, *Ex parte* 87
Harrison *v.* Barton 40
Haws *v.* Haws... 39
Heath *v.* Hubbard 94
Heckles *v.* Heckles 83
Henderson *v.* Eason 62, 78, 93
Hereward, The... 88
Hewett, *In re*, Hewett *v.* Hallett 44
Higgins *v.* Thomas 94
Hill's Case 26
Hill *v.* Hickin 80, 82, 83
Hinton *v.* Hinton 37
Hoban Deceased, *In re*, Lonergan *v.* Hoban 43
Hobbs, *In re* 24, 34
Hole *v.* Thomas 76
Horn *v.* Gilpin... ... ... 86, 96
Horsley and Knighton's Patent, *In re* 90
Hughes *v.* D'Arcy 47
Huntsman, The 88

In re Baker, Pursey *v.* Holloway 25
In re Barton's Will 43
In re Biss, Biss *v.* Biss 70, 83
In re Blaiberg and Abrahams 41
In re Brogden 31
In re Bryan, Godfrey *v.* Bryan 12
In re Buck, Bruty *v.* Mackey 103
In re Butler's Trusts, Hughes *v.* Anderson 43
In re Colling's Settled Estates 84
In re Cook's Mortgage, Lawledge *v.* Tyndale 81
In re David and Matthews 60, 61
In re Dixon, Byram *v.* Tull... 16
In re Green's Settlement 36
In re Greenwood's Trusts 24
In re Gue, Smith *v.* Gue 16
In re Harman and Uxbridge and Rickmansworth Railway Co. 41
In re Hewett, Hewett *v.* Hallett 44
In re Hoban Deceased, Lonergan *v.* Hoban 43
In re Hobbs 24, 34

PAGES

In re Horsley and Knighton's Patent 90
In re Jones, Farrington *v.* Forrester 81
In re Jupp 15
In re Leslie, Leslie *v.* French 82
In re March, Mander *v.* Harris 15
In re Marquis of Bute's Will 30
In re Mary Smith 77
In re Matson, James *v.* Dickinson... 23
In re Osborne and Bright's Ltd. 84
In re Plyer's Trust 30
In re Potter, *Ex parte* Parke 57
In re Selous, Thomson *v.* Selous 35
In re Smart, Smart *v.* Smart 22
In re Smith, Dew *v.* Kennedy 16
In re Thompson 32
In re Trustees of Fisher's Will 30
In re Waddell's Contract 30
In re Watts' Settlement 30
In re West and Hardy's Contract 41
In re Wilford, Taylor *v.* Taylor 43, 44
In re Wilks, Child *v.* Bulmer 43
In re Wilson, Wilson *v.* Holloway... 62
In re Woolley, Wormald *v.* Woolley 40
In re Wylde 15

Jackson *v.* Jackson 43, 61
Jackson *v.* Stopherd 65
Jacobs *v.* Seward 73, 80, 91–93
Jacomb *v.* Turner 48
James, R. *v.* 13
James *v.* Portman 45
Jeffereys *v.* Small 41, 60
Jeffereys *v.* Boosey 89
Jefferys *v.* Smith 75
Job *v.* Potton 77
Johnstone *v.* Faber 27
Jones, *In re*, Farrington *v.* Forrester 81
Jones *v.* Brown 94
Jope *v.* Morshead 47
Jupp, *In re* 16
Justice Windham's Case 36

Kay *v.* Johnston 82
Kennedy *v.* De Trafford 70, 78, 83
Kenny, R. *v.* 6, 13
Kent, The 85
Kenworthy *v.* Ward 33

PAGES

King *v.* Boys 32

Lake *v.* Craddock 60, 61
Lake *v.* Gibson 40, 60, 61
Lambert *v.* Rogers 72
Lancaster, Case of the Duchy of 106
Lauri *v.* Renad 58, 59
Law Guarantee Society *v.* Bank of England 31
Leigh *v.* Dickeson 70, 80, 81
Leslie, *In re*, Leslie *v.* French 82
Leslie *v.* Clifford 67
Lewis *v.* Langdon 60
Lindsay *v.* Gibbs 87
Lloyd *v.* Loaring 103
London Financial Association *v.* Kelk 97
Lord Abergavenny's Case 38
Lord Buckhurst's Case 72
Lord Mountjoy's Case 27, 70
Lord Wellesley *v.* Withers 45
Lyon *v.* Knowles 96, 97

McMahon *v.* Burchell 79
Manners *v.* Charlesworth 26
March, *In re*, Mander *v.* Harris 15
Marchant *v.* Cragg 15
Margaret, The 85
Marquis of Bute's Will, *In re* 30
Marryat *v.* Townly 40
Marshal *v.* Crutwell 38
Martin *v.* Crompe 60
Martyn *v.* Knowllys 76, 77
Mary Smith, *Re* 77
Marzials *v.* Gibbons 37
Mathers *v.* Green 89
Matson, *In re*, James *v.* Dickinson 23
May *v.* Harvey 57
May *v.* Hook 44
Mayfair Property Co. *v.* Johnston 46, 53
Mayhew *v.* Herrick 94
Mayor of Newcastle's Case 66
Meldon *v.* Abbot of Beaulieu 25
Mence *v.* Bagster 33
Meux *v.* Maltby 109
Milbank *v.* Revett 74
Morley *v.* Bird 39, 40, 51
Mountjoy, Case of Lord 27, 70
Moyse *v.* Giles 44

	PAGES
Mundy v. Mundy	46
Murphy v. Murphy	24, 34
Murray v. Hall	33, 73
Musgrave v. Dashwood	37
Mutton's Case	32
National Society etc. v. Gibbs	89
Newcastle, Case of Mayor of	66
Norris v. Caledonian Insurance Co.	82
Norton v. Frecker	26
Norwich, Case of Bishop of	52
Norwich Corporation v. Brown	108
Nyberg v. Handelaar	95
Oates v. Jackson	33
Ocle's Case	11
O'Hea v. Slattery	33
Osborne and Bright's Ltd., *In re*	84
Overall's Case	52
Owen v. Gibbons	25
Padwick v. Tyndale	34
Paine v. Wagner	14
Palmer v. Rich	43
Palmer v. Young	70
Parke, *Ex parte, In re* Potter	57
Parker v. Gerard	46, 53
Partriche v. Powlet	44
Paterson v. Mills	23
Payne, R. v.	13
Pemberton v. Barnes	26, 47
Petty v. Styward	40
Piercy v. Fynney	66
Pitt etc. v. Jones	48, 88
Plyer's Trust, *In re*	30
Pollok v. Kelly	13
Polyblank v. Hawkins	5
Porter v. Lopes	48, 75
Porter v. Porter	40
Potter, *In re, Ex parte* Parke	57
Powell v. Head	58, 70, 84, 89
Powis v. Smith	51
Prosser, Doe v.	73
Pullen v. Palmer	32, 50, 53, 56
Pulteney v. Warren	26, 96
Quarm v. Quarm	37

PAGES

R. *v.* Collector of Customs   60
R. *v.* James   13
R. *v.* Kenny 6, 13
R. *v.* Payne   13
R. *v.* Robson   64
R. *v.* Streeter 6, 13, 64
R. *v.* Tankard   64
Ramsay *v.* Margrett   15
Ramsden *v.* Fairthrop   76
Rector of Chedington's Case...   ...   .   11, 42
Richardson *v.* Feary   48
Rigby *v.* Connol   103
Rigden *v.* Vallier   39
Roberts *v.* Eberhardt   76
Roberts *v.* Holland 35, 56
Robertson *v.* Fraser   40
Robinson *v.* Preston   40
Robson, R. *v.*   64
Russell *v.* Men of Devon   109

Sammes' Case   33
Sanders *v.* Sanders   24
Sandford *v.* Ballard   74
Searle *v.* Smales   75
Selous, *In re*, Thomson *v.* Selous   35
Sheehan *v.* Great Eastern Railway Co. 57, 90
Shelley's Case   33
Shirt *v.* Shirt   23
Sleech's Case, Devaynes *v.* Noble   59
Sloman *v.* Government of New Zealand ...   .   ·108
Smallman *v.* Onions   77
Smart, *In re*, Smart *v.* Smart   22
Smith, *In re*, Dew *v.* Kennedy   16
Smith *v.* Kerr   103
Smith *v.* London and North Western Railway Co.   89
Smith *v.* Lyster   76
Smith *v.* Smith   30
Snelgar *v.* Henston   51
Standard Bank of B.S.A. *v.* Stokes   73
Staple *v.* Maurice   39
Stedman *v.* Smith   73
Steers *v.* Rogers   90
Sterling *v.* Penlington   50
Steward *v.* Blakeway   63
Story *v.* Lord Windsor   76
Stratton *v.* Best   33
Street *v.* Anderton   74

PAGES

Streeter, R. v. 6, 13, 64

Strelly v. Winson 86, 96, 97

Sturges v. Champneys   12

Sussex, Earl of, v. Temple 32, 33

Sutton v. Rolfe   50

Sutton's Hospital, Case of   102

Swan v. Swan 80, 82

Syms' Case   42

Taff Vale Railway Case 35, 109, 110

Tanistry, Le Case de   21

Tankard, R. v.   64

Taylor v. Midland Railway Co.   66

Taylor v. Neate   60

Teasdale v. Sanderson 81, 82

The Apollo   85

The Elizabeth and Jane   85

The Hereward   88

The Huntsman...   88

The Kent   85

The Margaret   85

The Vindobala   87

Thomas v. Thomas   78

Thompson, *In re*   32

Thompson v. Hakewill 50, 54

Thornley v. Thornley...   ...   .   13, 15, 16

Thornton v. Dixon 62, 63

Traherne v. Gardner 34

Trustees of Fisher's Will, *In re*   30

Tunbridge Wells Dippers' Case   55

Turner v. Major   60

Turner v. Morgan 53, 80

Twort v. Twort 76, 77

Tyson v. Fairclough   75

Venning v. Leckie   65

Vick v. Edwards   37

Vindobala, The   87

Waddell's Contract, *In re*   30

Walton v. Lavater 57, 89

Ward v. Ward 12, 30, 37

Warner v. Baynes   53

Warrington v. Warrington   14

Waterer v. Waterer   64

Waters v. Taylor   53

Watson v. Gray   74

PAGES

Watts' Settlement, *In re* 30
Waugh *v.* Land 56
Wellesley, Lord, *v.* Withers... 45
Wennhak *v.* Morgan 17
West and Hardy's Contract, *In re*... 41
Whaley *v.* Dawson 26
Wheeler *v.* Horne 78, 93
Wikes' Case 32
Wilkinson *v.* Hall 55, 56
Wilkinson *v.* Haygarth 73
Wilkinson *v.* Spearman 39
Williams *v.* Davies 38
Williams *v.* Hensman... ... ... 39, 42, 43
Williams *v.* Howarth 107
Willoughby *v.* Willoughby 74
Wilson *v.* Bell... 43
Wilson, *In re*, Wilson *v.* Holloway 62
Windham's Case 36, 51
Wing *v.* Angrave 36
Winterstoke Hundred's Case 55
Wiscot's Case 42
Wiseman *v.* Cotton 22
Woodroffe d. Doe d. Daniell 34
Woolley, *In re*, Wormald *v.* Woolley 40
Worrall *v.* Grayson 66
Wray *v.* Milestone 65
Wright *v.* Robotham 72
Wylde, *In re* 15
Wynne *v.* Styan 56

Yea *v.* Field 72
York *v.* Stowers 67
Young, *Ex parte* 87

CORRIGENDA.

p. 18, in line 11, *for* 1847 *read* 1897.

p. 33, in note 2, *for* Scratton *read* Stratton.

p. 46, in note 8, *for* Gerrard *read* Gerard.

CHAPTER I.

INTRODUCTION.

o " OWNERSHIP may be described as the entirety of the powers of use and disposal allowed by law[1]." In other words ownership contains three notable elements :—

    (*a*)   The power of enjoyment.

    (*b*)   The power of disposition during life or at death.

    (*c*)   The power of excluding others.

Jurisprudence may be expected to demand that everything shall have an owner: if any specific thing lacks an obvious owner, the law is likely to place the ownership thereof in the king.

Usually ownership is sole ownership. The general rule is simple—one thing, one owner. But there are exceptions. The owner's "power of excluding others" may be limited. The law, which recognises successive owners, may also—to respect certain situations in family relationship or in trade or otherwise —recognise simultaneous owners.

If two persons become concurrent owners of a shilling or of a ten-acre field, the law may decide to give them sixpence or five acres apiece, and so end the matter. But if the thing owned be difficult or impossible to divide, or if the collective ownership arises under conditions which forbid its complete severance into a mere set of sole ownerships, simplicity vanishes. Rules are needed to determine the rights of each co-owner as against his co-owners as well as against all other persons.

Sometimes co-ownership is concerned only with a small group of definite and ascertained persons, whose deaths it does not survive. In other cases the co-owners may compose a large

---

[1] Pollock, *First Book of Jurisprudence*, p. 166.

and vague body which purports to hold property successively
(in a kind of perpetuity which the law is likely to resent)
through infinite future generations of unascertained members.
The problem presented by these latter cases has been solved in
a remarkable way. Probably the most important groups of
co-owners (for example, groups of citizens, many religious and
commercial groups, schools, colleges, universities and hospitals)
are corporations. The process of incorporation begets a new
artificial person visible to the eye of the law. This person
holds the rights and property of the incorporated co-owners,
but remains so distinct from them that they can even make
contracts with it. By the creation of this representative
person, the group can be co-ordinated with other physical
persons in the legal system: it takes its place as a unit among
other units.

States have from time to time, for reasons of discipline or
revenue or out of respect for a particular theory, refused to
sanction the existence of so-called "corporate" bodies. The
principle of voluntary association has been obnoxious to
champions of the State or of the Crown[1]. Groups inevitably
claim attention as units: in England unity of the group has
been partly identified and partly confused with corporateness.
It has been orthodox for our lawyers to declare that corporateness is a privilege conceded by the king, a franchise which does
not exist without his consent, and an attribute which it is
unlawful for subjects to simulate without his authority. Consequently in England many groups of co-owners have failed to
attain the concession of corporateness; some (Nonconformists, for
example) were directly prevented, others found the formalities
too cumbrous and too costly.

Since the Companies Act of 1862 an easy road to cor-

---

[1] See Dicey, *Law and Opinion in
England*, App. n. 1, p. 465. See in
France the abolition of corporations in
the years 1791-4 (*Cambridge Modern
History*, VIII. 726), and compare the
language used in advocating the recent
Associations Bill. Compare also the Roman repression of *collegia* (Mommsen,
Römisches Staatsrecht, Bd III. 1180-1)
and the punishment of "adulterine"
gilds in England (Madox, *Firma Burgi*,
p. 26). I have dealt with this subject
more fully elsewhere (*General Principles of the Law of Corporations*,
c. xiii.).

porateness has been opened to groups[1]. But this method is scarcely fifty years old : co-owning bodies, when debarred from the privilege of incorporation, have had to content themselves with such protection as the trust afforded. By means of the trust it was possible to give nominal ownership to definite individuals (machinery being devised for replacing these individuals as they died or needed to be removed), while substantial ownership was given to the group. Like the idea of corporateness, the idea of trusteeship contains something fictional. If A, the nominal owner, holds property in trust for $B + C + D$ as beneficial owners, the ownership of A as against $B + C + D$ is a mere sham. As against strangers, however, A's ownership is real enough in law : A is not a mere agent for $B + C + D$; A is the legal owner. How valuable the English trust-system has been for the purposes of group-ownership, Professor Maitland has abundantly shown[2].

The title of the present essay precludes us from discussing collective ownership by corporation or by means of the trust. We therefore turn to consider other possible forms of collective ownership, and begin with that of husband and wife.

---

[1] 25, 26 Vict. c. 89, s. 6. By a mere process of registration. "Any seven or more persons" may thereby " form an incorporated company, with or without limited liability."

[2] *Political theories of the Middle Age*, translator's Introduction, pp. xxix.-xxxi.; *Township and Borough*, p. 16.

CHAPTER II.

MAN AND WIFE[1].

No group of collective owners is so closely knit as that group which consists of man and wife. They have a common life, and consequently common needs and liabilities which require to be met out of some kind of common property.

It is a frequent feature of marriage systems that a woman at her marriage contributes whatever property she may have to the satisfying of the needs of the pair; this property the husband, as head of the household, manages and controls. There is, however, great diversity in the conditions under which this property is held. Is a married man to dispose freely of the property of himself and his wife? Or does he need her assent? And, if so, how is that assent to be established? What property is to be liable for their debts? Further, when one of the pair dies, what distribution is to be made of the property which the husband has hitherto controlled? And what rights in the property of a dead *conjux* are to belong to the survivor?

The answers to these questions differ not only in different times and place, but even in the same time and place. Von Waechter, dealing with early Würtemberg, says that any attempt to distinguish its conflicting systems (in respect of the questions already mentioned, and without reference to minor divergences) would have to take account of more than sixteen different kinds[2].

---

[1] See Pollock and Maitland, *History of English Law*, Bk II. c. vii. s. 2. See also Stobbe's *Familienrecht* (Edn. 1900) which forms the fourth volume of his *Deutsches Privatrecht*.

[2] Cited in Stobbe, *loc. cit.* p. 90, n. (3).

The Civil Code of France recognises community of property between husband and wife where they have no written ante-nuptial settlement[1]. In England, however, there is no such general *communio bonorum* between man and wife, either in fact or in name. At our common law the lands belonging to a wife at her marriage or afterwards acquired vested in the husband during the marriage. It matters little whether the seisin in such lands was understood to be in the husband in right of the wife, or in the husband and wife in right of the wife[2]. Neither case was a case of community. Of movable things belonging to the wife the husband at the common law was entitled to the fullest possession.

Naturally the fact of common use has suggested common ownership. Setting aside some specific objects, such as the husband's armour or the wife's jewels, which are owned more exclusively than other things which are in common use, we might suppose that there was a general opportunity for the law to adopt the idea of a *communio bonorum*. The incidents of married life need not require the appropriation of specific articles to one or other of the *conjuges*. Dissolution of marriage of course makes a difference. It may be that the wife will be allowed at her death to dispose not merely of her personal attire, but also of her reasonable proportion (a half or a third as the case may be) of the chattels[3]. Moreover if a wife may not, or does not, make a will, her share of the chattels may descend at her death in one of several ways. For example in the eleventh century Strassburg received the following law:—
quicumque...legitimam uxorem accepit,...si eam mori contigerit sine filiis eorum amborum, vir suae uxori succedat et monia bona

---

[1] Article **1401**. See *Encycl. of Laws of England*, *s.v.* Community of Property.

[2] See Polyblank *v.* Hawkins (1780), Douglas' Rep. I. 329. Co. Litt. 299, 326. As to chattels real, see Litt. ss. 526, 665: Bacon's *Abridgment*, "Baron and Feme" (B).

[3] Bracton says that though she can-not make a will without her husband's consent, it may be allowed *propter honestatem* as a concession to her character. *Receptum est quandoquidem quod testamentum facere possit de rationabili parte quam habitura esset si virum supervixisset et maxime de rebus sibi datis et concessis ad orna-mentum quae sua propria dici poterunt, sicut de rebus et jocalibus.* f. 60 b.

ejus percipiat[1]. On the other hand, in Scotland (until fifty
years ago) the wife's share descended to her children, or failing
them, to her own folk[2]. Professor Maitland suggests that in
England the Churchmen would have considered that the wife's
share should be distributed, in spite of the claims of the living,
for the good of her soul. But, as he explains, at the beginning
of the thirteenth century the ecclesiastical courts assumed
control of the succession to movable things. The common law
thenceforth dealt with the rights and goods of man and wife
only so long as the marriage endured. Debarred from considering the state of affairs which might ensue upon the
dissolution of the marriage, common law had no hesitation in
confirming the husband in his absolute power over things
movable[3].

Collective ownership of the chattels of man and wife was
thus not received into our common law. Yet the possibility of
its reception is sometimes indicated. At common law a wife
could not be indicted for stealing the goods of her husband[4].
This rule of law is usually explained as founded upon the con-
ception that man and wife are not twain but one flesh[5], *un
person en ley*[6]. According to Bracton, *vir et uxor sunt quasi
unica persona, quia caro una et sanguis unus*[7]. But this
metaphor did not induce the law to favour community of goods.
Bracton continues:—*Res licet sit propria uxoris, vir tamen
ejus custos, cum sit caput mulieris*; if our early lawyers had
any notion to explain the relation of the husband to the
property of the wife, it was probably this notion of guardian-
ship[8]. Other notions might have had influence. There was the

[1] Cited in Stobbe, IV. p. 121. See
also s. 304, p. 297.

[2] See Fraser, *Husband and Wife*, pp.
662, 977, 1528: and *L. Q. R.* 10, p. 346,
"Difference between English and
Scotch Law," by J. A. Lovat-Fraser.

[3] La femme naveit nule propriete en
les chateus vivant son baron. Y. B.
32–3, Edw. I. 187.

[4] R. v. Streeter, 64 J. P. 537: R. v.
Kenny, 2 Q. B. D. 307. Archbold,

Criminal Pleading, 23rd Edition,
p. 550.

[5] See Genesis ii. 23–4. Matt. xix.
4–6. Mark x. 6–9, etc.

[6] Co. Litt. 112 a: "Inasmuch as the
husband and wife be one person, the
land cannot be parted by moities." 350.

[7] Bracton, lib. 5, tr. 5, c. 25. See
Cahill v. Cahill, 8 App. Cas., at p. 425.

[8] Compare the language of Bracton
cited in Pollock and Maitland, II. 414.

similar notion to which Bracton refers, a notion founded upon scriptural authority, that the husband is the head of the wife. The subjection of the wife is still a feature of our criminal law, and the incapacity of the wife in matters of property is but lately removed. There might have been also a lingering notion that the husband by paying a "bride-price" had become entitled to the wife and all her belongings. As far as English law is concerned, these speculative theorisings do not lead far; modern metaphysics may increase confusion. In Germany, however, Stobbe has not shirked the attempt to analyse the ownership of husband and wife. Dealing with schemes of family law which are certainly more communistic than ours, he discusses several theories[1].

I. *The man as single owner.* Supporters of this view assert that the woman has only an eventual right, a right which does not exist until the dissolution of the marriage. This view is based principally on the right of the man to dispose of the property and to charge it with his debts, although this right is of course restricted occasionally by the requirement that the wife should assent to his disposition of the property. This theory may not suit Germany, but it might have served well enough for England.

II. *The pair as owners with aliquot shares.* This view is said in Germany to find favour with those who are anxious to establish the fact of Roman influence. The contract of marriage was supposed to create a *societas* between man and wife *quapropter etiam omnia per eos constante matrimonio et quamdiu simul habitarunt, acquisita veniunt communicanda et aequaliter dividenda.* Later, marriage was supposed to create a community of property held by husband and wife in theoretic proportions. The proportion might be one-half or two-thirds to the husband, or corresponding to such division as would take place at the dissolution of the community. If we assume that they have such a half share, we get the result that the husband controls his own half by virtue of his ownership and his wife's

Nec aliquid inde habuit nisi racione custodie puerorum suorum et heredum uxoris sue. Notebook, 1771. Non *habet inde nisi custodiam. Ib. 1774.*
[1] *Deutsches Privatrecht,* IV. p. 268.

half by virtue of his marriage. It might be said that by
marriage each *cónjux* gives up half his or her property, and in
return takes half the property of the other. The position is
of course profoundly affected by the fact that the husband
represents the pair; and it becomes complicated according as
the laws allow *conjux A* to hamper *conjux B* in the disposal of
not only *B*'s but also of *A*'s share.

To this suggested system of joint ownership with aliquot
shares Stobbe objects that neither husband nor wife can during
marriage insist on partition. There is also the difficulty that
on the dissolution of the marriage the survivor may take less
than he or she had before. Further, the proportion is not
always certain or unalterable. It is latent; it may vary according as it is the husband or the wife who dies first, and
according as there is no child, or one child, or more, at that
death. Stobbe thus passes on to the third theory.

III. *The pair as owners without aliquot shares.* If the
husband alone is not the owner (and ownership by the wife
alone need not be here considered) and if the husband and wife
do not own in an ascertainable proportion, they must be collective owners with indefinite and undivided shares. This view is
developed in various ways.

(*a*) It is possible to postulate a juristic person composed
of husband and wife but separate and indistinguishable from
them. This is to secure for the group which is composed of
husband and wife a form of representation and of unity similar
to that which is secured for the Corporation in England. In
fact if we made a juristic person of the husband and wife in
England, we should probably call it (as we have generally called
the various legal persons which differ from mere physical persons,—e.g. the parish priest, the bishop, the king, the hospital,
the university, the borough and the limited company) a corporation. A legal *persona* would be created to hold the rights and
property of the pair, acting probably through the husband as its
representative or agent; as a separate person, husband and wife
would be able to contract with either husband or wife. The
death of one of the pair would dissolve the juristic person, and
cause its property to descend in whatever manner, or to whatever

heirs, the law might allow. Debts incurred by the pair would be debts of the juristic person[1], and it would be understood that each *conjux* on marriage gave up his or her property to an entirely new and artificial entity.

(*b*) By a variation of this theory, the pair might be supposed to be a single person but not a separate person, a fellowship but not a corporation, something which should stand to the complete juristic person as a partnership in England stands to a limited company. The distinction is one which appeals to German jurists, and it is confirmed by Beseler[2], who was a pioneer of the school of supporters of a German—as opposed to a Roman—theory of corporate life[3]. The husband and wife are a unit; their personalities merge in one personality, but not so as to create an independent *persona* with rights and duties of its own. The pair in fact become not a *universitas*, but an organism acting by its organs which are the husband and the wife.

(*c*) The husband and wife have also been compared to the German institution of the "united hand[4]." This group (which Dr Gierke traces back to the group of brothers who in early family law were left as co-heirs on the death of the father of the family) was originally a unit symbolically bound by the clasped hand in the pursuit of some common purpose or duty. Seen from without, it is a single person with rights and duties; seen from within, it is a collective person with a group-will which is the will of all and which does not allow itself to be over-ruled by the will of its head.

If the group composed of husband and wife be comparable to the group of the "united hand," the position stands thus:— neither husband nor wife is either owner of the whole property, or part owner of a definite share. He or she may have a share,

[1] Subject to some *ultra vires* doctrine being developed for the protection of the juristic person, as in our law of corporations.

[2] *Volksrecht und Juristenrecht*, p. 169.

[3] See Professor Maitland's Introduction to *Political Theories of the Middle Age* (translated from Dr Gierke, who dedicated his work to Beseler), pp. xviii. etc.

[4] Gemeinschaft zur gesammten Hand. See Gierke, *Das deutsche Genossenschaftsrecht*, II. 923: *Deutsches Privatrecht*, I. 663.

but the share need not be determined; for, while the marriage endures, the only thing to be considered is that the property belongs to both husband and wife together, just as if they were not two persons but one "subject." While the marriage endures, neither of the two appropriates a portion of the common property, but each within his or her appointed limits can dispose of what is common to both. In this disposal sometimes both must unite, sometimes one may act with the consent of the other, sometimes one (probably in important matters the husband, and in minor household affairs the wife) can act singly. Where one of the two can thus act independently, the power of disposal is not limited to his or her share, but extends to the whole and is binding on both.

It might be possible to fit to this theory the community which has existed between man and wife in Scotland. "According to the nature of society," wrote Lord Stair, "there is a communion of goods between married persons,...but so that through the husband's economical power of government, the administration during the marriage of the whole is alone in the husband[1]." But the language is not always precise; nor is the idea of community thoroughly established in Scotland. It appears to have found its way from Germany into Scotland by way of the Scotch students who studied in Paris; nor was it received in Scotland without protest[2].

(d) The remaining possibility suggested by Stobbe is that of a united ownership wherein each of the two is owner of the whole under conditions described as *condominium plurium in solidum*. In the words of the earliest supporter of this theory *sic utriusque conjugis bona confunduntur, ut quivis eorum totius patrimonii in solidum dominus sit, et quae uxoris fuerint, jam et ejusdem et mariti sint: vicissim quae maritus habuerit, jam sua et uxoris suae sint, uno verbo et maritus et uxor jure dicere*

[1] *Institutions* I. 4, 9.
[2] See Fraser, *Husband and Wife*, c. ix. The author doubts if community existed in Scotland much before Lord Stair's work appeared in 1681. He cited the following comment made in 1683:—"There is no exact society and communion of goods between the husband and wife; but only *analogicè, impropriè* and *abusivè*: there being no communion at all as to the property, but only during the marriage there is a resemblance of a communion *quoad usum.*" *Ib.* p. 664.

*potest, "totum patrimonium meum est*¹.*"* The fact that such *condominium in solidum* is contrary to Roman principles² is far from an offence to modern German jurists. There is a more solid objection to be found in the argument that, if this theory be accepted, the surviving *conjux* must inevitably in all cases be owner of the whole property;—which in Germany is not always the case.

We have in England a form of tenancy by husband and wife which suits this theory, without being open to the same objection; for under it the surviving *conjux* takes the whole property³. This form of tenancy, which is more truly a collective ownership than any other ownership by husband and wife in English law, is called "Tenancy by Entireties." It arises, in Coke's words, "where the husband and wife are joyntly seised to them and their heires of an estate made during the coverture⁴." They would thereby obtain a kind of *condominium plurium in solidum*; they take, it is said, *per tout et non per my* : each has the whole estate : there are no moieties between them⁵. Consequently when either of the two dies, the other remains seised of the whole estate by reason of the original limitation rather than under any right of survivorship. Thus it is that no alienation or partition by the husband or wife in such a case will defeat the interest of the survivor⁶. "The husband alone cannot, without joining his wife, devest the estate of the wife⁷." As is shown in *Ocle's Case,* the wife's survivorship was undefeated even when her husband had been attainted and executed for high treason⁸.

In respect of a term of years or other chattel real, the husband has, according to Preston, a power of assigning during his wife's life⁹. In *Grute v. Locroft*¹⁰ (where, however, it is not

¹ Justus Veracius, cited in Stobbe, IV. p. 279.

² Duorum in solidum dominium esse...non posse. D. 13. 6. 5. 15.

³ See Foster, *Joint Ownership and Partition of Real property,* c. vi.

⁴ Co. Litt. 326 a.

⁵ Co. Litt. 187, 299 b. Dyer 9, 23, and 19, 36.

⁶ Co. Litt. 326 a : Back *v.* Andrews,

2 Vern. 120: Green d. Crew *v.* King, 2 Bl. 1211.

⁷ Lord Kenyon C.J., in Doe d. Freestone *v.* Parratt, 5 Term Rep. at p. 654. See 3, 4 Will. IV. c. 74.

⁸ Co. Litt. 187 a.

⁹ 2 Abstr. 57.

¹⁰ Cro. Eliz. 287 : discussed in Rector of Chedington's Case, 1 Co. Rep. 155 a.

expressly said that husband and wife were tenants by entireties), it was held that a husband may make a lease of lands held jointly with his wife to commence after his death, and it will be good though the wife survive. "As regards money and chattels," says Mr Challis, "the husband alone can give a good discharge therefor, and can alienate after reduction into possession ; and the wife has no equity to a settlement thereof[1]." Ordinarily if a husband came into a Court of Equity to seek assistance to obtain the benefit of his wife's property, the Court would withhold its assistance until it had secured to the wife the means of subsistence[2]. There is a dictum of Chief Baron Richards, in *Attorney-General v. Bacchus*[3], suggesting that this equitable principle extends to the case of a tenancy by entireties. Moreover in *Atcheson v. Atcheson*, where husband and wife were tenants by entireties and the husband had assigned their interest to a stranger to secure a sum of money, the Court protected the wife to some extent by preserving her right by survivorship and by retaining the fund in Court with a direction to pay the dividends to the husband during the joint lives, with liberty for the survivor to apply[4]. The law was fully reviewed in *Ward v. Ward*. In that case Thomas Wise, at the marriage of his daughter Helen to Henry Ward, covenanted with trustees to pay to them during his life an annuity of £60 ; the trustees were to stand possessed thereof upon trust to pay the same "unto and to the use of the husband and wife during their joint lives," with trusts over for the survivor and for the children of the marriage. It was held that there was a tenancy by entireties under which the whole of the annuity was payable to the husband and passed to his judgment creditor, and that the wife was not entitled to claim her equity to a settlement out of any part of it[5]. This decision was followed by *In re Bryan, Godfrey v. Bryan*[6]. In *Chamier v. Tyrell*[7], where a trust was held to create a tenancy by entireties, it was decided that arrears of interest,

---

[1] *Real Property*, p. 345. See 2 Prest. Abstr. 39 : Co. Litt. 351.

[2] See the judgment in Sturgis *v.* Champneys, 5 Mylne and Craig, 97.

[3] 9 Price, at p. 40.

[4] 11 Beav. 485.

[5] 14 Ch. D. 506.

[6] *Ib.* 516.

[7] 1894. 1 Ir. Rep. 267.

accrued in the life of the husband, belonged to his estate and could not be considered as choses in action of the wife not reduced into possession by the husband.

The foundation of a tenancy by entireties is the fact of marriage. A conveyance to a husband and wife as joint tenants would (before the Married Women's Property Act, 1882, to which reference will be made later) have created a tenancy by entireties[1]. On the other hand a man and woman holding as joint tenants, do not by subsequent intermarriage become tenants by entireties; they continue to hold "by moieties[2]." If the marriage of tenants by entireties be dissolved by a decree absolute, they become joint tenants[3]. A woman may thus become entitled to an account of rents and profits from her former husband, as from the date of the decree, under the statute of Anne, by which joint tenants have this remedy[4].

The fact of marriage produced the fiction of the legal unity of husband and wife. In consequence of this unity, at common law a wife could not steal her husband's goods[5]. For the same reason husband and wife could not have conveyed to each other, apart from the Statute of Uses[6]. And a limitation to H (a husband), W (his wife) and X (a third person) was a limitation not to three persons but to two. X would take one-half, H and W would take the other as tenants by entireties[7]. If H, W and X hold as joint tenants and do not sever the joint tenancy, X will take the whole estate upon the death of H and W; if X die first, the whole estate will vest in H and W or the survivor of them.

"The rule of English law that a gift to a man and his wife, and to a third person, is to be construed as a gift of a moiety to

[1] Pollok v. Kelly, 1856, 6 Ir. C.L. Rep. 367.

[2] Co. Litt. 187 b: Green dem. Crew v. King, 2 Bl. 1211.

[3] Thornley v. Thornley, 1898, 2 Ch. 229.

[4] Ib. See 3, 4 Anne, c. 18, s. 2.

[5] 1 Hale, 514. She can now be convicted only by virtue of the provisions of the Married Women's Property Act, 1882. See Archbold, Criminal Pleading (23rd Edn. 1905), pp. 443, 459, 460, 550: R. v. Kenny, 2 Q.B.D. 307: R. v. Streeter, 1900, 2 Q.B. 601: R. v. James, 1902, 1 K.B. 541: R. v. Payne, 1906, 1 K.B. 97.

[6] Litt. s. 168.

[7] Co. Litt. 187 a.

the husband and wife and a moiety to the third person is founded
on the doctrine of English law that husband and wife are, for
most purposes, one person. And yet any indication, however
slight, of an intention that each shall take separately has been
held to defeat the application of this doctrine[1]." The following
cases illustrate the history and nice application of the rule. In
Lewin v. Cox, in 1599, Popham C.J. observes that if there be a
devise to a husband and wife and a third person "equally," they
are tenants in common each taking a third: where otherwise
(i.e., presumably, in the absence of the word "equally") the
husband and wife would take a moiety between them[2]. In
1684, in *Bricker v. Whatley*, there was a residuary bequest to
R. B., C. B., and S. W., and H. his wife, equally to be divided
amongst them. It was held that S. W. and H., husband and
wife, took one joint share and not two separate shares. Stress
was apparently laid by the Lord Keeper on the occurrence of the
word "and" before the names of husband and wife, and on the
fact that the wife only (and not her husband) was of kin to the
testator[3]. In a copyhold case in 1690 (*Back v. Andrews*), a
surrender to J. A. and his wife and Elizabeth his daughter and
their heirs was held to give one moiety to J. A. and his wife,
and the other to Elizabeth[4]. In a much later case, *Attorney-
General v. Bacchus and others*, there was a residuary bequest to
"my son-in-law G. B., and my daughter P. his wife, for their
absolute benefit." In deciding the incidence of legacy duty, it
was held that the bequest was to the benefit of each to the
amount of one-half[5]. In *Warrington v. Warrington* (1842), a
bequest of property "equally between my brother T. W., my
sister A. V. C., my nephew W. H. W. and E. his wife, their heirs
and assigns" was held to give W. H. W. and E. one share each
and not merely one share together[6]. In 1849, in *Atcheson v.
Atcheson*, a bequest "to A., his wife and children," there being

[1] Dias *v.* de Liviera, 5 App. Cas. at pp. 135–6.

[2] Moore's Rep. 558.

[3] 1 Vern. 232. See Warrington *v.* Warrington, 2 Hare, at p. 56. It is there noted that in Littleton's illustrations of the rule the husband and wife are named first among the recipients.

[4] 2 Vern. 120.

[5] 1821. 9 Price 30: 11 Price 547.

[6] 2 Hare 54. See also Paine *v.* Wagner, 1841, 12 Sim. 484.

three children, was construed to divide the legacy into four
shares of which the husband and wife together took one[1]. In
In re Wylde there was a bequest of £100 "unto and amongst
J. C. and Catherine his wife, and W. L.," the cousin of the
testator "in equal shares and proportions." (In another part of
the will testator gave separate legacies of £200 each to J. C., C.
his wife and W. L.) The Court, considering the argument of
equal weight each way, allowed the *prima facie* interpretation
to prevail, and gave one moiety to the husband and wife and
the other to W. L.[2] In *Marchant v. Cragg* (1862) a bequest
"equally between my brother W. S. and his wife J. and my
sisters M. M. and S. S." was construed to give W. S. and J. not
a joint third but a separate fourth part apiece[3]. In the case of
Dias v. de Liviera (1880), where the Roman-Dutch law was
concerned as well as the English, the foreign law was applied,
under which husband and wife are treated as separate persons[4].
At this stage in its history, the principle under discussion was
complicated by the passing of the Married Women's Property
Act, 1882. Thenceforward a married woman was capable of
acquiring, holding and disposing of any property as her separate
property in the same manner as if she were a *feme sole*[5]. The
wife's separate interest was thereby recognised in any case where
a limitation would previously have created a tenancy by entireties. Nevertheless the single personality of husband and wife
survived the Act. In 1884 in *In re March, Mander v. Harris*,
where a testatrix gave estate to C. J. M. and J. H. and E. his
wife "to and for their use and benefit absolutely," Chitty J.
decided that the estate was divisible into thirds. The Court of
Appeal, however, held that, as the will was made before the
Married Women's Property Act came into force, it must be construed according to the law at that time; therefore the husband
and wife were together given one moiety[6]. Further, in 1888,

---

[1] Beav. 485. Also Gordon *v.* Whieldon, *ib.* 170.

[2] 1852. 2 De G.M. and Q. 726.

[3] 31 Beav. 398.

[4] 5 App. Cas. 123.

[5] 45, 46 Vict. c. 75, s. 1 (i). As to
the effect of this, see judgment of

Romer J. in Thornley *v.* Thornley,
1893, 2 Ch. at pp. 233–4, and of Lord
Esher, M.R., in Ramsay *v.* Margrett,
1894, 2 Q.B. at p. 25. See also Earle
v. Kingscote, 1900, 2 Ch. 585.

[6] 27 Ch. D. 166.

in the case of *In re Jupp*[1], where an estate was left between
testator's sister "M. B., D. B. her husband, and H. B. her step-
daughter in equal parts," it was held that M. B. and D. B. her
husband took each a fourth part, while H. B. took one-half.
M. B.'s share was to be her separate property under the Act.
This decision has met with considerable criticism[2]. In *In re
Dixon, Byram v. Tull* (1889)[3], a testator bequeathed the residue
of his estate to W. B., E. B. his wife, S. B., J. B., G. D. B., C. C.,
and C. C. his wife "to be equally divided between them share
and share alike." Each of the seven persons named was held
(as each might have been held even before the Married Women's
Property Act) entitled to a separate seventh share. In constru-
ing a will which contains a bequest to husband and wife as
inter alios members of a class, the Court gives separate shares to
each of them[4]. So, in *In re Smith, Dew v. Kennedy*[5], a testator
left residue to all his nephews and nieces living at his decease,
with a gift over to the children of nephews and nieces who
should die in his lifetime, such children to take in equal shares
which their respective parent would have taken if he or she had
survived the testator. There were twenty-three nephews and
nieces including two, James and Sarah, who afterwards inter-
married and died before the date of the will, leaving several
children. Kekewich J. held that the estate was divisible into
twenty-three shares of which the children of James and Sarah
were entitled to two.

The result of the passing of the Married Women's Property
Act is to substitute a joint-tenancy between husband and wife
for a tenancy by entireties wherever this latter form of co-
ownership would formerly have arisen[6]. Tenancy by entireties
rested on the fiction of the unity of man and wife,— a notion
which has survived the Act. If husband and wife are sometimes
still to be counted one person as between themselves and third

[1] 39 Ch. D. 148.

[2] See *Law Quarterly Review*, 4, p.
485, 6, p. 234.

[3] 42 Ch. D. 306.

[4] In re Gue, Smith *v.* Gue, 1842,
W.N. 88.

[5] 1892, W.N. 106.

[6] See Thornley *v.* Thornley, 1893,
2 Ch. 229: Challis, *Real Property*
(1892 Edn.), pp. 345–6, Goodeve, pp.
233–4.

parties, they must in future as between one another be counted two persons. In spite of a *dictum* in *Chamier v. Tyrell*[1], this principle of the single personality of husband and wife still holds a place in our law[2]. Its place however was undermined and made precarious by the Married Women's Property Act, and it is doubtful whether it is not now less help than hindrance.

Collective ownership of husband and wife as tenants by entireties is disappearing. Husband and wife, however, may also be co-owners either as joint tenants or as tenants in common. With these two forms of co-ownership we shall deal later.

[1] 1894, 1 Ir. Rep. at p. 271.

[2] For instance, an indictment for conspiracy can be brought against two persons, but not against husband and wife, 1 Hawksh. c. 72, s. 8. Compare also the rules of evidence. Even in a civil action for libel, disclosure of the libel by defendant to his wife is not publication : Wennhak *v.* Morgan, 20 Q. B. D. 635. The principle (like that under which the coercion of the wife by her husband is presumed in certain criminal cases) may often make for public policy and domestic peace; it is not however an absolute or universal feature of our law. See Crawley, *Husband and Wife*, pp. 32–3.

CHAPTER III.

CO-HEIRS.

THE English institution of primogeniture obstructs co-ownership. When a man dies intestate and leaves behind him property and a family, sole ownership may easily become collective ownership. That is the moment when laws must decide whether the property shall descend to one or to many, whether it shall be partible or impartible.

The process of succession is either "singular" or "universal." Property is either distributed piecemeal on the death of the intestate, or else it devolves in its integrity. The latter case will better satisfy the dead man's creditors. As the Land Transfer Act of 1847 indicates[1], it is convenient that there should be some one individual to occupy the position of the dead man and to carry on his *persona*. This convenience suggested to the Romans the personification of the inheritance itself,—*haereditas personam defuncti sustinet*[2].

We are used to expect that upon an intestacy the heir will be a man rather than a woman, and one man rather than several. Such a scheme of succession happens to favour the identification of heir with ancestor[3]. But if there be—as in many times and places there has been—a scheme of succession by several co-heirs, these co-heirs may constitute one single person for the purpose of sustaining the dead ancestor's *persona*. They need not be a completely developed juristic person in the sense in which a corporation is in England a distinct and single person :

[1] 60, 61 Vict. c. 65.
[2] D. 41. 1. 34 : cf. D. 46. 1. 22 : personae vice fungitur. See Bracton, ff. 8 a, 44 a : haereditas est in loco defuncti domini.

[3] See Y.B. 20, 21 Ed. I. 233. See further, Maine, *Ancient Law*, c. vi. on the Early History of Testamentary Succession : O. W. Holmes, *Common Law*, pp. 342–4.

they may be merely a disintegrable and imperfect unit in the sense in which our partnerships are units. But because of the oneness of their right, they will be treated as one person :— *plures cohaeredes sunt quasi unum corpus propter unitatem juris*[1]. English acceptance of primogeniture was not absolute. Attributed by some to far-off customs which required the first-born son to undertake a kind of domestic priesthood at his father's death[2], primogeniture was fostered by the military needs of feudalism ; it succeeded because it was simple. But, though simple, it was arbitrary and even unjust[3]. If the tangled cults of ancestor-worship, household-gods-worship, per-petual-fire-worship and hearth-worship required a single son to perform their traditional rites, a custom of devoting thereto not the oldest but the youngest son deserved equally to prevail. Usually it is the Esau, the first-born, who has the privileged birthright; but often the Benjamin, the latest-born, is the favourite. Instances of "Junior-right" occur widely[4]. Professor Maitland has shown us how in Norman days at Nottingham, side by side with the French custom of primogeniture, there was noted a native custom of ultimogeniture which has since been known as "borough-english[5]." Whether we explain the preference of the youngest son on the grounds that he is the

---

[1] Bracton, 76 b., cf. 66 b : haeredes propinquiores esse possunt plures sicut unus, et cuilibet jus descendit quasi uni haeredi propter juris unitatem. Cf. also *Notebook*, 1273 : cum omnes sint quasi unus haeres.

[2] See the *Laws of Manu*, IX. 105. Compare the Greek πρεσβεία, and see Le droit d'aînesse discussed by Coulanges, *la Cité Antique*. See H. E. Seebohm. *Structure of Greek Tribal Society*, cc. 1—2. The whole subject is fully treated in Cecil's *Primogeniture*.

[3] See the views attributed by Starkey to Pole, *England in the Reign of Henry VIII.* (E.E.T.S.), c. iv. See also Smith, *De Rep. Angl.*, bk. III. c. 7.

[4] In Brittany and elsewhere : see

Elton, *Origins of English History*, pp. 187–200 : Robinson on *Gavelkind* (4th edn.), bk. II. c. x. A great English example occurs in the manor of Taunton Dean : Collinson, *Somerset*, III. pp. 233–4. The burgesses of Leicester in 1255 successfully peti-tioned that primogeniture be substi-tuted for ultimogeniture in that town, "which, because of the powerlessness and tender age of the heirs, was going to ruin and manifest decay." See Bateson, *Records of Leicester*, I. 49–51.

[5] See Y.B. 1 Ed. III. f. 12 : see *Encycl. of Laws of England*, *s.v.* Borough English : Pollock and Mait-land, *History of English Law*, II. p. 279.

"hearth-side" child[1], or the child most dependent upon the home, or the child whose life is most likely to defeat the claims of feudal lords, or whether on mere grounds of natural affection[2], the principle of ultimogeniture has been as fully recognised as that of primogeniture. Neither of the two principles is so remarkable as the system of impartible inheritance upon which each depends.

Apart from schemes of succession which favour particular sons, there are some which are non-preferential. Under patriarchal conditions the sons' families may grow up together under the father's roof, as in the Homeric picture of Troy. In Priam's palace

πεντήκοντ' ἔνεσαν θάλαμοι ξεστοῖο λίθοιο
πλησίον ἀλλήλων δεδμημένοι· ἔνθα δὲ παῖδες
κοιμῶντο Πριάμοιο παρὰ μνηστῆς ἀλόχοισιν.

Priam's fifty daughters lived hard by[3]. Under this system of the joint and undivided family—which has many parallels in the East—each son on marrying seems to have built for himself not a new house but a new chamber in the old[4]. More information as to the size of the joint family in early German communities would probably furnish a further analogy[5]. Under such a system the death of the ancestor may leave the children in co-ownership with or without partibility. In classical times there was division among co-heirs at Athens[6]. In ancient

---

[1] See Robinson, *Gavelkind*, p. 234 (b), for a Mongolian custom connecting the youngest son with hearth-rites. Relics of hearth-worship are rare in Germanic communities, but the hearth is nevertheless the symbolical centre-point of the heritage. See Pollock and Maitland, *ib.* pp. 257–8. See below, p. 21, n. 6.

[2] Propter majorem patrum affectionem quam saepe erga postnatos filios suos habere solent. Glanville, vii. c. 1. See, generally, the discussion in Vinogradoff, *Growth of the Manor*, pp. 314–5: Robinson on *Gavelkind*,

pp. 28–9, 234–6.

[3] *Iliad*, vi. 244.

[4] Archaeological discovery seems to confirm this. See *Iliad*, xvii. 36, and Dr Leaf's note on both passages.

[5] See Heusler, *Inst. des deutschen Privatrechts*, i. 229. As to English family ownership, see Vinogradoff, *Growth of the Manor*, p. 142.

[6] See Seebohm, *op. cit.* p. 90: Demosthenes, s. 1055: Petitus, *Leg. Att.* vi. 6 : ἅπαντας τοὺς γνησίους υἱοὺς ἰσομοίρους εἶναι τῶν πατρῴων. See Cecil, *Primogeniture*, p. 12.

Germany, according to Tacitus, co-heirs succeeded by classes[1]. The Gortynian laws and the laws of ancient Wales[2] and Ireland[3] also bear witness to practices of collective succession. So does the Norman institution of parage, which, as it appears in Domesday, seems to show a stage between co-heirship and primogeniture, a stage in which a tenement descended intact to several heirs of whom one (probably the eldest) was representative and responsible for services due to king or lord[4].

In England collective ownership by co-heirs (who are called parceners or co-parceners, and are said to hold in co-parcenary) occurs in two ways:—

(a) Where primogeniture is upset by the proof of some special custom such as Kentish gavelkind.

In Kanc' in Gavelkynde the Fader to the Bough and the Sone to the Plough et ibidem omnes heredes masculi participant hereditatem similiter omnes feminae sed feminae non participant cum masculis[5].

Professor Maitland considers the expression "the Sone to the Plough" is a corrupt form of "the Sone to the Lowe[6]," the "lowe" being the "aster" or hearth to which reference has already been made[7]. "The Fader to the Bough" is usually explained as an allusion to the custom by which gavelkind lands are free from escheat upon judgment of death for felony[8]. By other rules

[1] *Germania*, c. 20. See also Elton, *Origins of English History*, p. 201.

[2] See Stat. Walliae, 12 Ed. I. : Welsh gavelkind, confirmed by 27 Hen. VIII. c. 26, s. 35, was by 34, 35 Hen. VIII. c. 91, assimilated to English tenure. See Co. Litt. 175 b, 176 a.

[3] Irish gavelkind is described in Sir John Davys' *Reports* (1628), 49–50, where see also Le Case de Tanistry, 28–42. See the same writer's *Discovery of the True Causes why Ireland was never entirely subdued*, p. 169.

[4] See the instances and comment in Maitland, *Domesday Book and Beyond*, p. 145 and notes : Pollock and Maitland, *History of English Law*, II. pp. 263–4,

276, and notes : Vinogradoff, *Growth of the Manor*, pp. 206–7.

[5] Stat. de Prerog. Regis, 17 Ed. II. c. 16. See Co. Litt. 14 a, 140 a : Litt. s. 265. For the incidents of gavelkind, see Robinson on *Gavelkind*, Bk. II. *passim*, and pp. 205–6.

[6] See Pollock and Maitland, *History of English Law*, I. p. 187, n. 2 ; II. p. 271, n. 4 : Bracton, *Notebook*, 1644.

[7] See above, p. 20, n. 1.

[8] See Blackstone, *Comm.* II. 84. The custom did not extend to high treason, Robinson on *Gavelkind*, pp. 180–1. See Bracton, 276 b : Dyer's Rep. 310 b.

incidental to this form of tenure, "the tenant is of age sufficient
to aliene his estate by feoffment at the age of fifteen," and "in
most places he had a power of devising lands by will, before the
statute for that purpose was made[1]." Further, in the case of
gavelkind lands, the dower is of a moiety, but ceases on re-
marriage or incontinence; and tenancy by the curtesy is of a
moiety, ceasing on re-marriage but attaching without birth of
issue[2]. The custom of gavelkind may require to be specially
pleaded and proved. "It behoveth in the declaration," says
Littleton, " to make mention of the custom[3]." Gavelkind, with
its Saxon and anti-feudal peculiarities, though not exclusively a
Kentish custom, is (for reasons which are not very clear[4])
principally found and asserted in Kent.

(b)   At the common law "where a man or woman seised of
certaine lands or tenements in fee simple or in taile hath no
issue but daughters and dieth, and the tenements descend to
the issues, and the daughters enter into the lands or tenements
so descended to them, then they are called parceners, and be
but one heire to their ancestor[5]."

The rule of primogeniture does not apply to women except
by the vagaries of local custom[6]. When an ancestor dies intestate without a male heir, two or more daughters take together
as parceners; a single daughter would of course be an heir and
not a parcener[7]. If two daughters and no male heir be left and
if a third daughter be born posthumously, the three take in co-
parcenary. If one of the three daughters dies leaving a family
of four daughters, these four grandchildren represent their

[1] See Blackstone, *ib.* As to alienation
at fifteen years of age, see Y.B. 3 Ed. II.
(Selden Society, 20) at pp. 159–162.

[2] See *Encycl. of Laws of England*,
s.v. Gavelkind; and, generally, Robinson on *Gavelkind*.

[3] S. 265. See Co. Litt. 175 b: Y.B.
21 Ed. IV. 57 b: 22 Ed. IV. 32 b:
Wiseman *v.* Cotton (1675), 1 Sid. 135:
In re Smart, Smart *v.* Smart, 18 Ch.
D. 165, and numerous cases cited by
Robinson, pp. 38–41.

[4] See Pollock and Maitland, *History*

of English Law, I. pp. 186–8: Vinogradoff, *Villainage in England*, p. 205.

[5] Litt. s. 241.

[6] See Watkins on *Copyholds*, for examples of various customs: *e.g.* descent
to eldest son of eldest daughter, if any
(Marden, Hereford), II. 501: to eldest
daughter in default of sons (Isle of
Man), II. 495: to youngest son, in
default to youngest daughter (Chelten-
ham), II. 485: also Rider *v.* Wood,
1 K. and J. 644.

[7] Litt. s. 242.

mother and together hold as one parcener in co-parcenary with
their two aunts. The descent is *"ratione stirpium* and not
ratione capitum, for in judgment of law every daughter hath a
several stock or root[1]." At common law when a parcener died
intestate, her estate passed entire to her heirs. This position
was unaffected by the Inheritance Act, 1833[2]. On the death
of a co-parcener, co-heiress of the purchaser of land, her son,
notwithstanding s. 2 of that Act, stands in her place *quoad* her
share[3]: this rule applies also in favour of her more remote lineal
descendants[4].

Coke distinguishes parceners by custom, whose unity is a
unity of inheritance, from parceners at common law, whose unity
is one of person[5]. Thus parceners in gavelkind are not *quasi
unus heres et unum corpus sed diversi heredes*[6]. On the other
hand, daughters holding as common law parceners have a
personal unity: *quanque files els sont, els sont parceners, et sont
forsque un heire a leur ancestor*[7].

The daughters are as one heir: here then was an opportunity
for jurists to place the several ownerships in a single "subject,"
and thus create out of a number of physical persons one single
"ideal" or "moral" person[8]. But no one went so far as to
introduce into the law of co-parcenary that idea of the *persona
ficta* which was so important in the development of the notions
about corporate bodies. The co-parceners "be but one heire,
and yet severall persons": they have "one entire freehold in the
land, so long as it remains undivided, in respect of any stranger's
praecipe. But betweene themselves to many purposes, they

---

[1] Co. Litt. 164.
[2] 3, 4 Will. IV. c. 106. As to s. 4,
see Shirt *v.* Shirt, 1879, W.N. 33.
[3] See Paterson *v.* Mills, 19 L.J.,
Ch. 310 : Cooper *v.* France, *ib.* p. 313.
[4] See In re Matson, James *v.*
Dickinson, 1897, 2 Ch. 509. See
Williams, *Real Property,* Appendix B.
[5] Co. Litt. 176 a.
[6] Bracton, f. 428. As to co-heirs of
a peerage, see Beaumont Peerage Case,

Cruise, 214.
[7] Litt. s. 241: Co. Litt. 163 b. Compare Y.B. 20 Ed. I. 233, where Cecily,
Agnes and Edith entered as daughters
and one heir. See also *ib.* 200.
[8] Other synonyms are persona arti-
ficialis, persona civilis, persona intel-
lectualis, persona imaginaria. See
Dr Gierke, *Althusius,* p. 193, n. 195 :
Deutsches Privatrecht, I. 9. 470, n. 6.

have in judgment of law severall freeholds[1]." They are said to be "seised jointly" within the meaning of the Trustee Acts[2]. The possession of one of two parceners was formerly the possession of the other[3]. The law, however, has been altered by the Real Property Limitation Act, 1833[4].

Co-parceners are plainly not one person in law. If *A* dies intestate, and leaves *B* and *C*, his daughters, as co-parceners, the death of *B* does not give the full estate to *C* by any right of survivorship. There is some evidence that the *jus accrescendi*[5] may have once existed between parceners[6], but the right of the survivor never established itself fully in our law. Further if *B* were attainted for felony, *B's* share would escheat[7]. The holding of co-parceners is undoubtedly several, for one of them can enfeoff another[8]. It is a holding by entireties *ubi omnes simul et in solidum heredes sunt*[9], yet not by entireties because at any moment any parcener can obtain partition[10]. Unlike the shares of husband and wife, the shares of parceners are aliquot shares, fixed and definite. Of several sisters who are co-parceners, each has a direct right to *rationabilis pars sua inter sorores suas*[11].

As parcenary occurs only by descent, if two sisters purchase lands or tenements, they become not parceners but joint tenants

[1] Co. Litt. 164 a. See Tindal, L.C.J., in Decharmis *v.* Horwood, 4 Moore and Scott at pp. 404–5. The right of parceners to sue separately is there discussed.

[2] In re Greenwood's Trusts, 27 Ch. D. 359.

[3] See the argument in De la More *v.* Thwing, Y.B. 2 Ed. II. (Seld. Soc. 17), at p. 178.

[4] 3, 4 Will. IV. c. 27, s. 12. See Burroughs *v.* McCreight, 1 Jo. and Lat. 290: Murphy *v.* Murphy, 15, 1 r. C.L.R. 205 : Sanders *v.* Sanders, 19 Ch. D. 373 : In re Hobbs, 36 Ch. D. 553.

[5] See below, p. 35. There being no survivorship between parceners, the

incidents of curtesy and dower obtain.

[6] See Pollock and Maitland, *History of English Law*, II. pp. 246 and 291 or 7.

[7] Co. Litt. 163 b.

[8] Co. Litt. 164 a : or convey by release, Co. Litt. 200 b : or by grant, 8, 9 Vict. c. 106, s. 3.

[9] Bracton, 76 b.

[10] See above, p. 11, as to husband and wife. Littleton derives the name parceners from the partibility of the estate : s. 241.

[11] See for example, as early as 1200, in *Select Civil Pleas* (Selden Society, 3), Vol. I. cases 6, 16, etc. See *Codex Dipl.* I. 300, for an instance of partition in A.D. 833.

or tenants in common[1]. And so a limitation "to the use of the right heirs of *A*," who were three sisters and the five daughters of a deceased sister, was held to create a joint tenancy and not a co-parcenary[2]. When by partition a co-parcenary is dissolved, the several owners continue entitled by descent and not by purchase[3].

Co-parcenary may be determined in a number of ways, by the physical partition of the estate, or by the severance of the unity of title.

I. For example, the unity of title among parceners is severed if one parcener alienates her share[4]. The alienee does not hold in co-parcenary. So, if two parceners marry, have issue and die, their husbands do not hold in co-parcenary[5]. And if the ownerships of several co-parceners coalesce in the ownership of one, the parcenary is of course at an end[6].

II. Voluntary partition could take place

(*a*) By parol agreement at common law. Either the parceners agreed upon the division, or they accepted a division by arbitrators (the parceners choosing their shares in order of age), or else the eldest sister made the division, the younger sisters having first choice of shares[7]. A deed is now (except in the case of copyholds) necessary[8], though equity might be satisfied by an agreement in writing within the Statute of Frauds to make partition.

(*b*) By lot. Littleton gives quaint directions for inscribing the parts of the land secretly upon "a little scrowle" which is "covered all in waxe in manner of a little ball"; the balls are

[1] Litt. s. 254.

[2] Berens *v.* Fellows, 1887, W.N. 58. The "right heirs" took as *personae designatae*. See also Re Baker, Pursey *v.* Holloway, 79 L.T. 343 : Owen *v.* Gibbons, 1902, 1 Ch. 636.

[3] Doe dem. Crosthwaite *v.* Dixon, 5 A. and E. 834. See Savile, 113.

[4] Co. Litt. 167 b, 174 a, 243 b : Litt. s. 309. See argument in Meldon *v.* Abbot of Beaulieu, Y.B. 2 Ed. II. (Selden Society, 17), p. 120. The remaining co-parceners continue to hold their shares in parcenary.

[5] Co. Litt. 167 b : Litt. s. 264.

[6] Y.B. 3 Ed. II. (Selden Society, 20), pp. 65–7, contains a case where Olive and Agnes, two parceners, made a joint alienation. Olive died, and Agnes disputed the alienation as having been under age.

[7] Litt. ss. 243–5, 250.

[8] 8, 9 Vict. c. 106, s. 3. See precedents in *Encycl. of Forms and Precedents*, IX. pp. 425, etc.

" put into a hat to be kept in the hands of an indifferent man,"
and drawn out by each parcener in order of her age[1]. Coke is
content to illustrate the practice by the case of the division of
Palestine by lot amongst the children of Israel[2].

(c) By consent through the Board of Agriculture under the
Inclosure Acts[3].

III. Compulsory partition could take place

(a) At common law by the writ *de partitione facienda*,
whereby the sheriff, with a jury of twelve men *de vicineto*, made
personal inspection of the tenements in the presence of the
parties; having divided the estate equally, he assigned shares
to the co-parceners at his discretion[4]. This writ was abolished
by the Real Property Limitation Act, 1833[5].

(b) In Chancery. Apparently where co-parceners held of
the king *in capite*, Chancery claimed jurisdiction as to partition,
especially during the nonage of any parcener[6]. This jurisdiction
arose at first by writ of livery and partition (to be distinguished
from the writ *de partitione facienda*)[7]: but, being incidental to
tenure, it was presumably affected by the Statute of Tenures.
Afterwards Chancery exercised an equitable jurisdiction on a
bill filed praying for partition. This jurisdiction, the earliest
instance of which is difficult to date[8], continues to-day, subject
to modification by the Partition Acts[9]. The compulsory powers
of sale and partition by the Courts are discussed later[10].

[1] S. 246.

[2] Co. Litt. 167 a : Numbers xxvi.
55, xxxiii. 54.

[3] 8, 9 Vict. 118, s. 90. See, for
precedents of application to, and order
by, the Board, *Encycl. of Forms and
Precedents*, ix. pp. 452, etc.

[4] Litt. ss. 248–9 : F.N.B. 61 R :
Bracton, 75. As to redressing an unequal partition, see Dyer, 52 a, pl. 20 :
73 a, pl. 7. As to mesne profits upon
bringing a writ of partition between
co-heirs, see Drury v. Drury (6 Car. I.)
Rep. in Ch. 26 : see also Dean v.
Wade, *ib.* (16 Car. I.), Norton v. Frecker,
Pulteney v. Warren, 6 Ves. pp. 77, 91
etc.

[5] 3, 4 Will. IV. c. 27, s. 36.

[6] See F.N.B. 62 D : Prerog. Regis,
17 Ed. II. c. 6 : Hill's Case, Y.B.
21 Ed. III. M. pl. 14, f. 31.

[7] See Butler's note to Co. Litt. 169 a.
A difference between partition at law
and in equity is given in Whaley v.
Dawson, 2 Sch. and Lef. 371.

[8] See Manners v. Charlesworth,
1 Myl. and K. 330 ; and see below,
p. 47.

[9] See 3, 4 Will. IV. c. 27, s. 36 :
Judicature Act, 1873, s. 34 (3) : and
31, 32 Vict. c. 40 : 39, 40 Vict. c. 17.
See Hatherley, L.C., in Pemberton v.
Barnes, L.R. 6 Ch. 685.

[10] See below, pp. 47–8.

Of the rights which may fall to parceners some are entire and indivisible. Coke says estovers are indivisible[1]. "Such manner of profits cannot be partitioned; for if such an inheritance descend to divers heirs, one of them shall have the profits integrally, and the other sisters something in allowance[2]," If there be no fund from which such allowance can be made, the estovers may be taken alternately by each parcener, or for an equal period in turn. Similarly two parceners dividing an advowson should present alternately, or by lot[3]: if they cannot agree to present, the eldest has the right to present first[4]. Bracton considered sergeanties indivisible[5]; there is, however, in 1221 an instance which supports the opposite view[6].

In general, titles of honour or dignity lie in the discretion of the king. Public policy and military needs might prohibit the division of a castle between two or more parceners[7]. Consequently the title to an earldom, if it fell into parcenary, might remain in abeyance, or be given to one parcener at the king's will: "and this hath been the usage since the Conquest, as it is said[8]." Mr Round describes a case in which the Earl of Chester left three co-heirs. The son of one offered Richard I. 7000 marcs for the fief in 1191, and so won it. Being unable to pay, he had to resign the barony. The husband of another heir then offered the same sum and was accepted. The third co-heir was seemingly ignored[9]. In such a case it was sometimes sufficient to appoint a stranger as deputy, if he were a male of sufficient

[1] Co. Litt. 164 b, 165 a : see Lord Mountjoy's Case, Godbold 17.

[2] Bereford, J., in Y.B. 2 Ed. II. (Selden Society, 17), p. 58. See De la More v. Thwing, ib. at p. 178, as to the impartibility of a warren.

[3] Johnstone v. Faber : 6 D.M. and G. 439.

[4] Co. Litt. 166 b : Gully v. Bishop of Exeter, 10 B. and C. 584 : see Archdeacon Carowe's Case, Dyer 55 a, pl. 5. As to the position of co-owners of an advowson on partition, see 7 Anne, c. 18.

[5] Bracton, 77, 395 : see Pollock and

Maitland, *History of English Law*, I. 290, II. 275.

[6] Ib. II. 275, n. 4. As to homage by parceners, see Y.B. 2 Ed. II. (Selden Society, 17), pp. 78–9. As to fealty owed to parceners, see Y.B. 3 Ed. II. (Selden Society, 19), p. 103.

[7] See Bracton, 76 b : Co. Litt. 165 a.

[8] Co. Litt. 165 a. The matter is thoroughly discussed in Palmer, *Peerage Law in England* (1907), pp. 100–8, 110.

[9] Round, *Ancient Charters*, number 59.

dignity and satisfactory to the king[1]. The claims to the office
of Lord Great Chamberlain have caused considerable discussion
of the rule[2].

The dignity of the English crown is indivisible. If a king
died leaving two daughters, the elder daughter would inherit
the Crown as heir not as parcener. In the time of Henry VIII.
statute provided that, in default of male heirs to the king, the
crown was to go to the eldest issue female (Elizabeth) "as the
Crown of England hath been accustomed and ought to go in
cases where there be heirs female to the same[3]." *Regnum non
est divisibile.* Coke is content to cite Virgil on the Trojan
practice, but there was a case nearer home which might have
upset the rule. In 1293 Johannes de Hastynge *petit propartem
suam de regno Scotiae tanquam de haereditate partibili.* He
affirmed that the kingdom descended to John de Balliol, Robert
de Bruce and himself. Bruce agreed, although—as he was
reminded—he had previously recognised the said kingdom to
be impartible. Balliol, who disdained to claim a mere part, was
finally rewarded with the whole. But Edward I. and all his
council did not lightly come to this conclusion. The king left
two questions to his advisers:—

(i) *An regnum Scotiae sit partibile?* (ii) *Si idem regnum
non sit partibile, an escaetae et acquisita sint partibilia?* They
answered both questions in the negative; but the maxim *divide
et impera* might well have drawn a different decision from
the king[4].

Though a kingdom was impartible, a county could be
divided. Of the heirs of the Earl of Chester one claimed the
whole county, others wanted a division on the ground that equal
partition among sisters had always been the English practice.
Their claim succeeded: *consideratum est quod Comitatus divi-
datur inter praedictos participes[5].*

---

[1] Co. Litt. 165 a: Butler's note 8.

[2] See the claims in 1901–2 of the
Duke of Athol, Earl Carrington, the
Marquis of Cholmondeley and the Earl
of Ancaster.

[3] 25 Hen. VIII. c. 22, s. 7.

[4] See *Foedera*, I. pt. 2, pp. 779–780.

See a recent account in Huyshe, *Royal
Manor of Hitchin and the Balliols*,
c. xv.

[5] Bracton, *Notebook*, 1127, 1213,
1227. (See Maitland's edition, III.
p. 283 and notes.) See *De Legibus*, 76.

This ease of partition is the notable feature which distinguishes parcenary from tenancy by entireties. The case of the County of Chester shews that although all the parceners took as one heir (as is expressly stated in the judgment) the unity of co-parcenary has a precarious life and is readily disintegrated. Mention will be made in a subsequent chapter of the not too clearly defined rights of parceners *inter se*[1].

To sum up, co-parcenary does not arise unless there is (*a*) intestacy, and (*b*) either (i) an exceptional local custom, or (ii) the absence of a male heir and the presence of two more female heirs of the same degree. Thus, in Coke's words, " this inheritance of co-parceners is the rarest kind of inheritance which is in the law[2]."

---

[1] See below, Chapter VII.   [2] Co. Litt. 164 a.

CHAPTER IV.

JOINT TENANTS.

CO-PARCENARY always arises by descent, "which, coming by the act of law and right of blood, is the noblest and worthiest means whereby lands do fall from one to another[1]." We pass now to the case of joint tenants, whose ownership "cannot arise by descent or act of law, but merely by purchase or acquisition by the act of the party[2]." For this reason joint tenants were anciently called *participes et non haeredes*[3].

A joint tenancy may be acquired by the act of the party where two or more persons enter upon land and gain a title by prescription or by wrongfully disseising the freeholder[3]. So also where two persons, being lawfully in possession of a copyhold, continued in possession after their title had come to an end, it was decided in *Ward v. Ward*[4] that they held on as joint tenants.

A joint tenancy arises by purchase where there is a limitation of one estate *pro indiviso* to two or more persons by word, will or deed[5]. Co-owners by grant or devise without words of

---

[1] Co. Litt. 163 b.

[2] Blackst. *Comm.* II. 181. Joint tenancy may also arise by operation of statute, where trustees are appointed under the Trustee Act, 1850, s. 10 (see In re Marquis of Bute's Will, Johnson 15: in spite of doubts suggested in In re Watts' Settlement, 9 Hare 106: and In re Plyer's Trust, 9 Hare 220), and s. 34 (see In re Trustees of Fisher's Will, 1 W.R. 505: Smith v. Smith, 3 Drew. 72), or under

the Bankruptcy Act, 1869, s. 83 (see judgment of Bacon, V.C., In re Waddell's Contract, 2 Ch. D. 172), to hold as joint tenants.

[3] Co. Litt. 180 b.

[4] L.R. 6 Chanc. App. 789.

[5] The question what words will give a joint tenancy by deed or by will, is fully discussed in the notes to Morley v. Bird, Tudor's *Leading Cases* (4th edn.), pp. 271–7.

severance and without actual subsequent severance hold in joint
tenancy.   Coke observes that between such co-owners there is
a " two-fold privity : viz. in estate and in possession[1]."   Further,
it is usual to say that joint tenants have a fourfold unity—unity
of (*a*) Interest, (*b*) Title, (*c*) Time and (*d*) Possession[2].

(*a*)   Unity of Interest means that the estates of the joint
tenants are equal in quantity.   A demise to *A* and *B* for life,
or to *A* and *B* for a term of years, makes *A* and *B* joint tenants;
on the other hand a demise to *A* for life and to *B* for a term of
years creates no joint tenancy but a tenancy in common[3].
Tenancy in common is the loosest form of plural ownership in
an undivided estate ; it will be discussed in the next chapter.

Unity of Interest means further that joint tenants must be
equal in capacity.   Coke and Littleton discuss cases in which a
body politic or corporation (their instances refer chiefly to
corporations sole not aggregate) is co-owner with a natural
man.   " If lands be given to an abbot and a secular man, to
have and to hold to them, viz. to the abbot and his successor
and to the secular man to him and to his heires," the donees
are not joint tenants but tenants in common[4].   On the other
hand lands given to a bishop and a layman to have and to hold
to them two and their heirs (the bishop taking in his natural
and not in his official capacity) are held in joint tenancy[5].   In
respect of chattels real or personal, also, an abbot and a secular
man, or a bishop and a secular man, might be joint tenants
because " no chattel can go in succession in a case of sole
corporation[6]."   Apart from these exceptions, however, king and
subject[7], parson and layman, corporation and natural man, could
not be joint tenants together for they had no unity of interest[8].

[1] Co. Litt. 169 a.
[2] Blackst. *Comm.* II. 180.
[3] Co. Litt. 188 a.
[4] Litt. s. 297.
[5] Co. Litt. 190 a.
[6] Co. Litt. 190 a.   The explanation is given in Co. Litt. 46 b: but there were exceptions.   See Butler's note (2) to Co. Litt. 190 a.
[7] The king, taking *in jure coronae*, is not equal in capacity to the subject. But see 21, 22 Vict. c. 94, s. 50, which provided for the case of manors held in joint tenancy or co-parcenary with the Crown.
[8] See Bennett *v.* Holbeach, 2 Wms. Saund. at p. 716, n. 1: Law Guarantee Society *v.* Bank of England, 24 Q.B.D. 406 : In re Brogden, 1888, W.N. 238.

This principle of law has been changed by the Bodies Corporate (Joint Tenancy) Act of 1899. " A body corporate shall be capable of acquiring and holding any real or personal property in joint tenancy in the same manner as if it were an individual." A corporation and an individual, or two or more corporations, can now hold property as joint tenants[1].

Certain disabilities were formerly attached to aliens and attainted persons. Before the Naturalisation Act, 1870[2] (which was not retrospective) an alien holding as joint tenant with another person was subject to the right of the Crown to seize the alien's moiety upon office found[3]. A joint tenant convicted of treason or felony would have forfeited his moiety to the Crown at common law; statutes have now abolished such forfeiture[4].

(*b*) "Joyntenants must come in by one title[5]"—that is to say, by one and the same instrument or act.

(*c*) Unity of Time means that the estate of all the joint tenants must arise simultaneously. If there be two co-owners whose moieties have vested at different times, they cannot be joint tenants. Coke mentions some possible exceptions to this rule. "If a man make a feoffement in fee to the use of himselfe and of such wife as he should afterwards marrie, for terme of their lives, and after he taketh wife, they are joyntenants, and yet come to their estates at severall times[6]. And so it is if I disseise one to the use of two, and the one agrees at one time, and the other at another, yet they are joyntenants[7]." The need that joint tenants should take simultaneously seems to be satis-

---

[1] 62, 63 Vict. c. 20, s. 1. In re Thompson, 1905, 1 Ch. 229. As to Consols see a previous Act, 55, 56 Vict. c. 39.

[2] 33 Vict. c. 14, s. 2.

[3] Co. Litt. 2 b, 42 b, and 186 a. King *v*. Boys, Dyer, 283 b. And see the discussion in 1 Leon. 47, 1 Ventr. 417, and Jarman on *Wills*, pp. 67–9: also 22, 23 Vict. c. 21, s. 25, which abolished the need of inquisition being taken or office being found.

[4] See Wikes' Case, Lane 45, where a lessee was attainted of the Gunpowder Treason : Hales *v*. Petit, Plowd. 257, a case of *felo de se*. See 13, 14 Vict. c. 60, ss. 15–6 : 33, 34 Vict. c. 23, s. 2.

[5] Co. Litt. 299 b, 189 a : see Pullen *v*. Palmer, 3 Salk. 207.

[6] Co. Litt. 188 a : 1 Rep. 101 a : Mutton's Case, Dyer 274 b, 339 b: see Earl of Sussex v. Temple, 1 Ld. Raym. at p. 312: Goodeve, *Real Property* (1906 edn.), pp. 230–1.

[7] Co. Litt. 188 a.

fied if the feoffees' interest arises at the same moment under the Statute of Uses; "but otherwise it is of estates which pass by common law[1]." Under a will, also, estates in joint tenancy may arise at different times. If there is a limitation to the use of the children of *A*, on the birth of one child the whole vests in him; on the birth of another, that one takes jointly with the former, and so on progressively as the children are born[2]. The same principle obtains in the case of personal property[3].

(*d*) Unity of Possession implies that the estates of the joint tenants must be equal in quality. *A* and *B*, if they are joint tenants, have an equal interest in the undivided whole of the estate. In other words they hold *per my et per tout*. Husband and wife in a tenancy by entireties take, as we have seen, *per tout et non per my*[4]: each has rights over the whole, but cannot claim rights over an aliquot share. But each of two joint tenants has not only rights over the whole property but also a definite right to an equal half share of it. Each holds all and yet holds nothing, for he holds all in common and nothing separately by himself[5]: "yet to divers purposes each of them hath but a right to the moitie[6]." "The one hath by force of the joynture the one moity in law, and the other the other moity." So says Littleton[7]: until alienation or forfeiture, however, there is no right to a specific aliquot share.

Blackstone describes the consequences of this "thorough and intimate union of interest and possession." "If two joint-tenants let a verbal lease of their land, reserving rent to be paid to one of them, it shall enure to both, in respect to the joint

[1] Sammes' Case, 13 Rep. 57. Kenworthy *v.* Ward, 11 Hare 196. See Gilbert on *Uses*, p. 71, Sugden's note 10, 3rd Edn. 1811.

[2] See Editor's note (Q. 3) to Shelley's Case, I. Rep. at 101 a : Oates, etc. *v.* Jackson, 2 Str. 1172: Scratton *v.* Best, 2 Brown Chanc. 233 : Hales *v.* Ridley, Pollexfen, 373 : Earl of Sussex *v.* Temple, 1 Lord Raym. 310: Amies *v.* Skillern, 14 Sim. 428.

[3] Mence *v.* Bagster, 4 De Q. and S. 162 : Kenworthy *v.* Ward, 11 Hare

196 : O'Hea *v.* Slattery, 1895, 1 Ir. Rep. 7.

[4] *Supra*, p. 11. See the judgment in Chamier *v.* Tyrell, 1894, 1 Ir. Rep. at p. 271. Manning's note to Murray *v.* Hall, 7 C.B. 455, suggests that the phrase *per my*, used of joint tenants' holding, means "not in the least." See Litt. s. 288. Bracton, l. 5, tr. 5, c. 26.

[5] Bracton, f. 430.

[6] Co. Litt. 186 a.

[7] S. 291.

C.

reversion[1]. If their lessee surrenders his lease to one of them, it shall enure to both, because of the privity or relation of their estate[2]. On the same reason, livery of seisin, made to one joint-tenant, shall enure to both of them: and the entry, or re-entry, of one joint-tenant is as effectual in law as if it were the act of both[3]." But in 1833 the Real Property Limitation Act altered the law.

"Where any one or more of several persons entitled to any land or rent as co-parceners, joint-tenants or tenants in common, shall have been in possession or receipt of the entirety, or more than his or their undivided share or shares of such land, or of the profits thereof, or of such rent for his or their own benefit, or for the benefit of any person or persons entitled to the other share or shares of the same land or rent, such possession or receipt shall not be deemed to have been the possession or receipt of or by such last mentioned person or persons, or any of them[4]."

The possession of land by one of two co-owners can thus no longer be considered the possession of the other: further the entry or re-entry of one can no longer be considered to vest the property in the other[5]. Nevertheless the fourfold unity which binds joint tenants still has potential importance. In estates in copyhold, "as joint tenants make together but one tenant to the lord, and a heriot being payable only on the death of a person who dies solely seised, no heriot is due until the death of the survivor of them[6]." Further, the admittance of one joint tenant on the court rolls of a manor is the admittance of all: and if one joint tenant die, the survivors or survivor do not require a new admittance, for they take no new estate[7].

---

[1] Co. Litt. 214 a.

[2] *Id.* 192 a.

[3] Blackst. *Comm.* II. 182. See Brook, *Abridg.* tit. *Entre Congeable*, 37–8. Co. Litt. 364. Doe d. Gill *v.* Pearson, 6 East 173.

[4] 3, 4 Will. IV. c. 27, s. 12.

[5] Woodroffe d. Doe d. Daniell, 15 M. and W. at pp. 792–3 : Murphy *v.* Murphy, 15 Ir. C.L. Rep. 205 : In re

Hobbs, Hobbs *v.* Wade, 36 Ch. Div. 553.

[6] Scriven on *Copyholds*, pp. 250–1. See Com. *Dig.* "Copyholds," K. 24. Padwick *v.* Tyndale, 1 E. and E. 184.

[7] Bence *v.* Gilpin, L.R. 3 Ex. 76 : see Traherne *v.* Gardner, 5 E. and B. 913. Watkins on *Copyholds*, I. 334, 338.

In spite of the fourfold unity, joint tenants are not a legal unit. If they appear in Court, they appear not as one person but as many[1]. In Coke's words, they must "jointly implead and be impleaded by others[2]," but this rule tends to be relaxed; the Rules of the Supreme Court order that "no cause or matter shall be defeated by the misjoinder or nonjoinder of parties[3]." Moreover "in all cases of actions for the prevention of waste or otherwise for the protection of property, one person may sue on behalf of himself and all persons having the same interest[4]." In *Broadbent v. Ledward*[5], where one of several joint owners (trustees of a club) brought an action for the detinue of certain pictures, Denman, L.C.J., decided against the defendant who had objected that the other joint owners should have been joined as co-plaintiffs. It is clear that of several joint covenantees one alone cannot sue on the covenant[6]. But if his fellow-promisees refuse to be joined as co-plaintiffs, after tender of an indemnity against costs, a joint promisee can add them as co-defendants for the purposes of maintaining an action on the contract[7].

Although joint tenants are not in law one person, their unity is strong enough to give them "the sole quality of survivorship which co-parceners have not[8]." "No survivor of other tenants *pro indiviso* shall have the whole by survivor, but only joyntenants: and this is called in law *jus accrescendi*[9]." It is conceivable that both of two joint tenants may die at the same

---

[1] See Stat. 34 Ed. I. Coke, 2 Inst. 527.

[2] Co. Litt. 180 b.

[3] Order XVI. r. 11. See Roberts *v.* Holland, 1893, 1 Q.B. at p. 667.

[4] R.S.C. Order XVI. r. 37.

[5] 11 Ad. and E. 209 : see also O. XVI. r. 9. Duke of Bedford *v.* Ellis, 1901, A.C. 18 : Taff Vale Railway Case, 1901, A.C. at p. 443. Compare also the cases of tenants in common, cited below, pp. 54–8.

[6] Wills, J., in Roberts *v.* Holland, 1893, 1 Q.B. at p. 667. See Foley *v.* Addenbrooke, 4 Q.B. 197.

[7] Cullen *v.* Knowles and Birks, 1898, 2 Q.B. 380.

[8] Co. Litt. 180 b. Litt. s. 280.

[9] Co. Litt. 1816. The right exists both in law and at equity. Aston *v.* Smallman, 2 Vern. 556. If an equitable tenancy in common and a legal joint tenancy equal and coextensive unite in the same persons, the former merges. "Two or more persons cannot be trustees for themselves for an estate coextensive with their legal estate." In re Selous, Thomson *v.* Selous, 1901, 1 Ch. 921.

moment, *e.g.* by shipwreck or earthquake. In such a case, according to Lord Thurlow, "the estate will remain in joint tenancy in their respective heirs[1]." The right of one joint tenant to take the whole estate by surviving the other may sometimes be valueless. If *A* and *B* are joint tenants for the life of *A*, *B* gains nothing by surviving *A*[2]. But in general the right of survivorship is important, though uncertain : moreover, the principle is found useful in the legal machinery of trust deeds. Trustees—that is to say, persons in whom the legal ownership of property is placed for the benefit of others—are made joint tenants. If one of several trustees dies, the legal ownership remains in the survivors; the representatives of the dead trustee obtain no interest in the trust estate, and have no power to meddle with its management.

Occasionally, by a conflict between this principle of survivorship and the terms of an instrument creating a joint ownership, a temporary joint estate may arise followed by a several inheritance. If *A* and *B*, being persons who cannot intermarry (*e.g.* brother and sister[3], or two men) are given lands to themselves and the heirs of their bodies, then *A* and *B* have a joint estate for their lives, the survivor takes by survivorship for his life, afterwards the issue of *A* and *B* (if any) take several inheritances[4]. If *A* and *B* can intermarry, "for the apparent possibilitie to marry, they have an estate tail in them presently. So it is where lands be given to the husband of *A* and to the wife of *B*, they have presently an estate in taile, in respect of the possibility[5]." If lands be given to a man and two women (or

[1] Bradshaw *v.* Toulmin, 2 Dickens, 633. Facts may establish that one of the two lived longer than the other. See Broughton *v.* Randall, Cro. Eliz. 502, where two joint tenants "were both hanged in one cart"; witnesses deposed that the younger lived longer, "as appeared by some tokens, viz. his shaking his legs." As to the presumption at law in such a case, see Wing *v.* Angrave (accident at sea), 30 L.J. Ch. 65 : In re Green's Settlement (Indian Mutiny Case), L.R. 1 Eq. 289.

[2] Co. Litt. 181 b, 193 a.

[3] 8 Rep. 87 a.

[4] Litt. s. 283. And see, generally, Justice Windham's Case, 5 Rep. 7–8 : Forrest *v.* Whiteway, 3 Ex. 367.

[5] Co. Litt. 20 b, 25 b. In a case where a testator devised a freehold estate to seven persons as "joint tenants, and not as tenants in common, and to the survivor of them, his or her heirs and assigns for ever," it was held that the effect of the devise was to make the devisees joint tenants for

conversely to a woman and two men) and the heirs of their bodies begotten, "in this case they have a joynt estate for life and every of them a severall inheritance, because they cannot have one issue of their bodies, neither shall there be by any construction a possibility upon a possibility, viz. that he shall marry the one first and then the other[1]." As we have already seen, a gift to *A* and *B* who are husband and wife, creates not a joint tenancy but a tenancy by entireties. On the other hand, a gift to *A* and *B* as joint tenants, remains a joint tenancy if *A* and *B* subsequently intermarry[2].

It will be noticed that joint tenancy differs from co-parcenary in the fact that its principles can be applied to the holding of goods as well as of lands. "If a horse or any other chattell personall be given to many, he which surviveth shall have the horse[3]."

The right of survivorship was strong enough to defeat a devise by a dying joint tenant. "The cause is, for that no devise can take effect till after the death of the deviser; and by his death all the land presently cometh by the law to his companion which surviveth, by survivor[4]." *Jus accrescendi praefertur ultimae voluntati[5]*. On the same principle, if a joint tenant died before carrying out an agreement to alien his part, the survivor could not be compelled at common law to carry out the agreement[6]. There was another maxim, *jus accrescendi praefertur oneribus*. If one of two joint tenants burdens the property with a rent-charge, "after his decease the grant of the

life with a contingent remainder in fee simple for the survivor. Quarm *v.* Quarm, 1892, 1 Q.B. 184. See Co. Litt. 191 a, with Butler's note (i) thereto: Vick *v.* Edwards, 3 Peere Wms. 371: Challis on *Real Property* (2nd Edn.), p. 336.

[1] Co. Litt. 25 b, 184 a.
[2] See above, p. 13. Co. Litt. 187 b.
[3] Litt. s. 281. Things personal "cannot be vested in co-parcenary because they do not descend from the ancestor to the heir." Blackstone, *Comm.* II. 399. There can be tenants by entireties of personal property: see Ward *v.* Ward, 14 Ch. Div. 506. As to survivorship in respect of the copyright of joint authors, see Marzials *v.* Gibbons, L.R. 9, Ch. App. 518.
[4] Littleton (who had to consider only the case of will under burgage custom), s. 287.
[5] Co. Litt. 185 b.
[6] Musgrave *v.* Dashwood, 2 Vern. at p. 63. But as to equity, see Hinton *v.* Hinton, 2 Ves. 631: Brown *v.* Raindle, 3 Ves. 257.

rent charge is void... He which hath the land by survivor shall hold the whole land discharged[1]." So also "if one joyntenant granteth a common of pasture, or of turbary, or of estovers, or a corody or such like, out of his part, or a way over the land, this shall not bind the survivor[2]." Even if one joint tenant in fee simple died indebted to the king, no extent could be made upon the land in the hands of the survivor[2]. Nor was such land liable, on the death of a joint tenant, to curtesy[3], or dower[4], or to a judgment debt[5]. In other words the interest of a joint tenant does not become assets for the payment of his debts when he dies. The Land Transfer Act, 1897[6], provides that "where real estate is vested in any person *without a right in any other person to take by survivorship,*" the estate is to devolve at his death upon his personal representatives. The italicised words exclude land held in joint tenancy from the Act, but do not exclude land otherwise held by co-owners who have not the *jus accrescendi.*

Where husband and wife have a joint banking account, the circumstances of the case must be considered in deciding whether the wife is entitled at her husband's death to the sum standing to their credit. In *Marshal v. Crutwell*[7] it was held that the opening of such a joint account was not intended to be a provision for the wife, but merely a mode of conveniently managing the affairs of the husband who was in failing health : consequently the wife was not entitled on the death of her husband. But in *Williams v. Davies,* where it was intended to make provision for the wife, the fund was held to be her absolute property on her surviving her husband[8].

To the general rule of survivorship there are exceptions. Doubtless it is sometimes a hardship that "if three joint tenants be in fee simple, and the one hath issue and dieth, yet they

[1] Litt. s. 286.
[2] Co. Litt. 185 a.
[3] Co. Litt. 183 a.
[4] Litt. s. 45 : see Broughton v. Randall, Cro. Eliz. 502.
[5] Co. Litt. 184 b : Lord Abergavenny's Case, 6 Rep. 78 b.

[6] 60, 61 Vict. c. 65, s. 1 (i). See Goodeve, *Real Property* (1906 Edn.), pp. 124, 244.
[7] 1875. L.R. 20 Eq. 328.
[8] 1864. 33 L.J.P. 127 : see Gosling v. Gosling, 3 Drew. 335 : Drummer v. Pitcher, 2 My. and K. 262.

which survive shall have the whole tenements, and the issue
shall have nothing[1]." It has been argued that "joint-tenancy
was an odious title in equity, there being no reason that, because
a man lived longest or had the better constitution, therefor he
should be entitled to the whole estate[2]." Similarly, in *Staple v.
Maurice*, joint tenancy was said to "let in a mischief never
dreamt of by the parties," leaving families to beggary[3]. On the
other hand, it was urged in that case that "if any of the joint
tenants have a bad opinion of their own lives, they may sever
the joint tenancy and destroy the right of survivorship, by a
deed granting their respective shares in trust for themselves, or
may enter into covenants not to take advantage of each other
by survivorship. But if the joint tenancy be not severed, it is
an evidence of intention in the party to submit to the chance
of survivorship, or of that supineness and neglect to which our
law affords no assistance[4]." This opinion was repeated in *Cray
v. Willis*[5] by Jekyll, M.R., who denied that there was "anything
unreasonable or unequal in the law of joint tenancy, each having
an equal chance to survive." In *Rigden v. Vallier*[6] it was
observed that, "if two men make a purchase, they are understood to purchase a kind of chance between themselves which
of them shall survive." Nevertheless Equity set itself to discourage the principle of survivorship by inclining away from
joint tenancies towards tenancies in common of which survivorship is not an incident. "It is clear the ancient law was in
favour of a joint tenancy," but "the Courts, seeing the
inconvenience of that, have been desirous, wherever they could
find any intention of severance, to avail themselves of it[7]."
"Anything which in the slightest degree indicates an intention
to divide the property must be held to abrogate the idea of a

[1] Litt. s. 280.
[2] Barker *v.* Giles, 2 Peere Williams, at p. 280. And see the hard case of Wilkinson *v.* Spearman in Cook *v.* Cook, 2 Vern. at p. 245.
[3] So in Haws *v.* Haws, 1 Atk. 524, it was said that joint tenancies "in-troduce inconvenient estates and do not so well provide for families."

[4] 4 Brown's *Parl. Cases,* at pp. 585–6.
[5] 2 Peere Williams, at p. 529.
[6] 2 Ves. Senr. at p. 258.
[7] Arden, M.R., in Morley *v.* Bird, Tudor's *Leading Cases,* 4th Edn. at p. 265. See Page Wood, V.C., in Williams *v.* Hensman, 1 J. and H. at p. 557.

joint tenancy[1]." Equity would not pronounce in favour of a joint tenancy "if there were any circumstances from which it could be collected that a joint tenancy was not in contemplation[2]." So "if two purchase, and one advances more of the purchase-money than the other, there shall be no survivorship[3]." And even where two or more purchase in equal shares under conditions which naturally create a joint tenancy, parol evidence may be admitted to prove an intention to exclude the *jus accrescendi*[4].

Equity withdrew the right of survivorship from cases of mortgage. "If two people join in lending money upon a mortgage, equity says it could not be the intention that the interest in that should survive. Though they take a joint security, each means to lend his own and take back his own[5]." "The idea must be that persons must be presumed to be less willing to speculate on their own survivorship in the case of a loan than in that of a purchase[6]." Equity in fact used to presume that where several mortgagees lent money, the money belonged to them severally. Hence the mortgagor, on paying the monies, would have been obliged to obtain a receipt and reconveyance from the personal representatives of any one of the mortgagees who had died, in respect of the share of the deceased. As mortgagees are often trustees, this was an awkward circumstance; consequently mortgages were made to contain a so-

---

[1] Lord Hatherley in Robertson *v.* Fraser, L.R. 6 Ch. at p. 699. See Joyce, J., In re Woolley, Wormald *v.* Woolley, 1903, 2 Ch. at p. 211.

[2] Grant, M.R., in Aveling *v.* Knipe, 9 Ves. at p. 443, approved by Page Wood, V.C., in Harrison *v.* Barton, 1 Johns. and H. at p. 295. See Fleming *v.* Fleming, 5 Ir. Ch. Rep. 129. See also the cases of executory trusts such as Marryat *v.* Townley, 1 Ves. Senr. 102.

[3] Where one person contributes all the purchase-money, there may be a resulting trust in his favour. See the decision (and the doubt of Knight

Bruce, L.J.) in Garrick *v.* Taylor, 31 L.J. Ch. 68; also the notes to Dyer *v.* Dyer in *Leading Cases in Equity*, 2 White and Tudor (7th Edn.), at pp. 810, 818, etc.

[4] Harrison *v.* Barton, *in loc. cit.*; where the admissibility of mere statements of intention is discussed. See Robinson *v.* Preston, 4 K. and J. 510.

[5] Arden, M.R., in Morley *v.* Bird, Tudor's *Leading Cases*, at p. 266. See Petty *v.* Styward (7 Car. I.), 1 Ch. Rep. 31: Lake *v.* Gibson, 1 *Abridgment of Cases in Equity*, 290.

[6] Page Wood, V.C., in Harrison *v.* Barton, 1 Johns. and H. at p. 287.

called Joint Account clause[1]. The mortgagees were said to be advancing the money on a joint account in equity as well as in law. Further, it was usually provided that the receipt of the mortgagees " or the survivor or survivors of them " should be a good discharge. Trustees usually lent money on mortgage as absolute owners; it was not convenient, and it was not the practice, for conveyancers to disclose the trust in the mortgage deed[2]. Nor did the Courts inquire as to the trust[3]. "It is well settled that the joint account clause, which is a device of conveyancers to keep trusts off a title, is not notice of a trust[4]."

In mortgages made since the Conveyancing Act of 1881, where money is expressed to be advanced by, or owing to, two or more persons on a joint account, the money is deemed to be money belonging to them on a joint account as between them and the mortgagor; and the receipt in writing of the survivors or survivor of them is a complete discharge for all money due, " notwithstanding any notice to the payer of a severance of the joint account[5]."

Perhaps the largest class of exceptions to the rule of survivorship is that which occurs under the law merchant, where two or more persons are engaged in joint trade. The custom of merchants to exclude survivorship was gradually extended to all cases of undertaking for joint profit and loss: it is therefore a part of our partnership law. At one time partnership articles contained express provision against survivorship; but it was held in *Jeffereys v. Small*[6] that this was unnecessary. With this class of exceptions we shall deal later in a

[1] See Elphinstone, *Introd. to Conveyancing*, pp. 164–6.

[2] Carritt *v.* Real and Personal Advance Co. 42 Ch. D. at p. 272.

[3] In re Harman and Uxbridge and Rickmansworth Railway Co. 24 Ch. D. 720. The case of In re Blaiberg and Abrahams, 1899, 2 Ch. 340, must be distinguished on the ground that there notice of the trust was inadvertently disclosed.

[4] Farwell, J., In re West and Hardy's Contract, 1904, 1 Ch. at p. 147.

[5] This is the law only in so far as a contrary intention is not expressed in the mortgage. 44, 45 Vict. c. 41, s. 61: see also s. 60. See, generally, Addison on *Contracts*, 10th Edn. p. 296.

[6] 1 Vern. 217.

separate chapter[1], for it seems inconvenient to describe partners
either as joint tenants or as tenants in common.

Severance of an estate in joint tenancy destroys its incidents
and creates a different kind of estate. Severance may occur
(*a*) by operation of law, or (*b*) by act of parties.

(*a*) If *A* and *B* are joint tenants for their lives, and *A*
obtains—by purchase or by descent—the reversion, the joint
tenancy is severed by operation of law[2].

(*b*) The act of the parties can sever a joint tenancy by
interference with the four unities. Thus, if *A*, a joint tenant
in fee with *B*, aliens his share to *C* in fee, *B* and *C* are not
joint tenants but merely tenants in common. *A* and *B* held
under one title; *B* and *C* hold under several[3]. But if there
are three joint tenants, *A*, *B* and *X*, alienation by *A* to *C* does
not disturb the joint tenancy and right of survivorship as
between *B* and *X*[4]. It was not always clear whether *A*, being
joint tenant with *B*, can sever the joint tenancy by aliening
something less than his whole share to *C*. Littleton was in a
dilemma, although Coke ascribes to him the view which he
himself confirms "that the joynture is severed for the time[5]."
In *Syms' Case*[6] "it was held by the Justices that if the joynt-
tenants be of a term, and the one grants parcel of the term to
a stranger, by this the jointure of all is severed."

Vice-Chancellor Page Wood thus summed up the means of
severance in *Williams v. Hensman*[7]. "A joint tenancy may be
severed in three ways: in the first place, an act of any one of
the persons interested operating upon his own share may create
a severance as to that share....Secondly, a joint tenancy may be

[1] See below, Chapter VI.
[2] Wiscot's Case, 2 Rep. 60 b : Bacon
Ab., *Joint Tenants*, I. 6.
[3] Litt. s. 292.
[4] Litt. s. 294.
[5] Co. Litt. 191 b. See Jenks,
Modern Land Law, p. 171 : Williams
v. Hensman, 1 J. and H. 546: Cowper
v. Fletcher, 6 Best and Smith at
p. 472.
[6] 1584. Cro. Eliz. 33. See Co.

Litt. 192 a, where it is explained that
a term for a small number of years is
as high an interest as for many more
years. See Butler's note (i) thereto.
See as to a lease of joint lands to
commence at lessor's death, Grute *v.*
Locroft, Cro. Eliz. 287, which is discussed in Rector of Chedington's Case,
1 Rep. 155 a.
[7] 1 J. and H. at p. 557.

severed by mutual agreement[1]. And, in the third place, there may be a severance by any course of dealing sufficient to intimate that the interests of all were mutually treated as constituting a tenancy in common. When the severance depends on an inference of this kind without any express act of severance, it will not suffice to rely on an intention, with respect to the particular share, declared only behind the backs of the other persons interested. You must find, in this class of cases, a course of dealing by which the shares of all the parties to the contest have been affected, as happened in the case of *Wilson v. Bell*[2] and *Jackson v. Jackson*[3]." The material question is whether or not the parties have treated the interest as a tenancy in common. It is even immaterial that they should have acted in ignorance of the fact that their interest was a joint tenancy[4].

Before the Married Women's Property Act, 1882, the marriage of a woman holding personal property as joint tenant severed the joint tenancy[5]. In *Palmer v. Rich*[6], it was held that the marriage of a woman holding freeholds or leaseholds as joint tenant does not sever her joint tenancy[7]; and further, that the granting of a lease by her husband and the other joint tenant, reserving the rent to the lessors jointly, does not necessarily effect a severance. In a previous case, *In re Butler's Trusts, Hughes v. Anderson*[8], it had been decided that the marriage of a woman holding joint tenant a chose in action (not reduced into possession by the husband) did not sever the joint tenancy[9].

We have already seen that an agreement by a joint tenant to sell would in equity sever the jointure[10]. Similarly a sever-

---

[1] See Frewen *v.* Relfe, 2 Brown, *Chanc. Cases*, 220: In re Wilford, Taylor *v.* Taylor, 11 Ch. D. 267.

[2] 5 Ir. Eq. Rep. 501.

[3] 9 Ves. 591.

[4] Williams *v.* Hensman, 1 J. and H. at p. 561. See also as to severance by conduct, In re Wilks, Child *v.* Bulmer, 1891, 3 Ch. 59.

[5] Co. Litt. 185 b: Bracebridge *v.* Cook, Plowd. 416.

[6] 1897, 1 Ch. 134.

[7] See, however, In re Hoban deceased, Lonergan *v.* Hoban, 1896, 1 Ir. R. 401.

[8] 38 Ch. Div. 286.

[9] See also In re Barton's Will, 10 Hare 12: Armstrong *v.* Armstrong, L.R. 7 Eq. 518.

[10] See above, p. 37, Brown *v.* Raindle, 3 Ves. 257.

ance would be effected by an agreement between two persons
about to marry, to settle property held by the woman as joint
tenant[1], or even afterwards acquired by her under a subsequent
instrument[2]. "*Alienatio rei praefertur juri accrescendi* is a
maxim in Equity," said the Lord Chancellor in *Partriche v.
Powlet*: "but then it must appear to be an actual alienation,
and not from inference or implication only, without any express
declaration of the parties[3]." In that case there was no agreement for the purpose and no actual alienation. "The declaration of one of the parties that (the estate) should be severed is
not sufficient unless it amounts to an actual agreement[4]." In
the case, *In re Wilford's Estate, Taylor v. Taylor*[5], two sisters,
who under a will were entitled as joint tenants to certain lease-
hold property, agreed to make mutual wills bequeathing it in
trust for each other for life with remainder to their nieces.
Wills were afterwards made according to the agreement. It
was held that the agreement severed the joint tenancy. It
should be added that there cannot be severance by will; *jus
accrescendi praefertur ultimae voluntati*[6]. Nevertheless in the
case of copyholds there is a possible qualification of this rule.
"Two joint-tenants copyholders in fee: the one surrenders into
the hand of two tenants to the use of his last will, and makes
his will of that land and dies." Upon these facts it was held in
Porter v. Porter[7] that the jointure was thereby severed. This
kind of dormant surrender is a severance, but it is revocable
during the life of the surrenderor[8]. In *Edwards v. Champion*[9],
where there was a surrender by a woman to the uses of her
husband's will, his will was not made till after her death. It
was doubted whether in such circumstances a surrender could
operate to sever.

A joint tenancy is of course destroyed if one joint tenant

[1] Caldwell *v.* Fellowes, L.R. 9 Eq. 410: Burnaby *v.* Equitable Reversionary Interest Society, 28 Ch. D. 416.
[2] In re Hewett, Hewett *v.* Hallett, 1893, 1 Ch. 362.
[3] 2 Atk. at p. 55.
[4] *Ib.* at p. 54: see also May *v.* Hook, Butler's note (i) to Co. Litt.
246 a: Moyse *v.* Giles, 2 Vern. 385.
[5] 11 Ch. Div. 267.
[6] See *supra*, p. 37.
[7] Cro. Jac. 100. See also Co. Litt. 59 b.
[8] Gale *v.* Gale: 2 Cox 136.
[9] 3 De G. M. and G. 202, at p. 216.

conveys his share to the other[1]. This conveyance is effected by release: no words of inheritance are necessary to pass a fee[2]. A grant was construed as a release[3]. In copyhold estates, "until the joint-tenants have been admitted, until they have acquired a legal title, there is no estate on which the release can operate[4]."

In *Cooper v. Fletcher* it was held that one of two joint tenants may demise to the other with the usual incidents of a reversion and a right to distrain[5]. The question was there raised also, whether one joint tenant can lease to another[6].

If, of three joint tenants *A*, *B* and *C*, *A* releases all his share to *B*, *B* and *C* will still be joint tenants of their original shares, but they will be tenants in common in respect of what was formerly *A*'s share[7].

Finally, severance of jointure can be effected by partition.

Joint tenants, if of full age, could make voluntary partition. Lands could be divided into separate shares to be taken in severalty by the several tenants; the partition was completed by entry. In this process a deed was, and is, necessary[8]. According to Littleton[9] a joint tenant could not be compelled by law to make partition. The writs mentioned by Fitzherbert seem to refer to local custom in London and elsewhere[10]. Coke, in qualifying Littleton's statement, says that "by the custome of some cities and boroughs one joint tenant or tenant in common may compell his companion by writ of partition grounded upon the custome, to make partition[11]." Early cases at the beginning of the thirteenth century show that the Justices were occasionally called upon to deal with partition

[1] Childs *v.* Wescot, Cro. Eliz. 470.

[2] Co. Litt. 273 b : as to feoffment, see 14 Viner *Ab.* 510.

[3] Eustace *v.* Scawen, Cro. Jac. 696: the grantee "shall be said in of the entire estate, as by the feoffment." See also Chester *v.* Willan, 2 Wms. Saund. 96 a.

[4] Bence *v.* Gilpin, L.R 3 Ex. at p. 82. See Lord Wellesley *v.* Withers, 4 E. and B. 750.

[5] 6 Best and Smith 464.

[6] *Ib.* at p. 469: see Co. Litt. 186 a ; and James *v.* Portman, Owen 102.

[7] Litt. s. 304.

[8] Co. Litt. 187 a. Could joint tenants make parol partition outside the county where the land lay? See Dyer 179 a, pl. 43.

[9] S. 290.

[10] *Natura Brevium*, 138 A and C.

[11] Co. Litt. 187 a.

claims. There are of course instances in gavelkind. For
example, one brother demands of another the fifth part of
certain land " as the reasonable portion which falls to him of
the inheritance of his father[1]." And in answer to another
similar demand, a tenant pleads that the estate, being a socage,
never was partitioned and ought not to be[2]. In 1202 there is
also an interesting action for partition of a wood which is held
in common by the parties[3]. Whether or not such cases support
the inference that common law gave joint tenants the right to
compel partition, at any rate this right was granted by statute
after Littleton ceased writing and before Coke began to comment[4]. According to the preamble of this Statute[5] no joint
tenant or tenant in common " by the law doth or may know
their several parts or portions in the same or that that is his or
theirs, by itself undivided, and cannot by the laws of this realm
otherwise occupy or take the profits of the same, or make any
severance division or partition thereof without either of their
mutual assents and consents"; and "oftentimes of their perverse
covetous and malicious minds and will against all right justice
equity and good conscience " joint owners have " extirpated
subverted pulled down and destroyed all the houses edifices
and buildings meadows pastures commons " etc., " to the open
wrong of others holding jointly or in common with them who
have always been without assured remedy for the same."
Therefore the common-law writ *de partitione facienda* (as
possessed by co-parceners[6]) was given to joint tenants and
tenants in common[7]. This writ was abolished when procedure
in Chancery had become more common[8].

In his Chancery Reports Tothill cites cases which show that

---

[1] *Select Civil Pleas I.* (Selden
Society, 3), case 6.
[2] *Ib.* case 61.
[3] *Ib.* case 121.
[4] Co. Litt. 187 a. See Mundy v.
Mundy, 2 Ves. at p. 125.
[5] 31 Henry VIII. c. 1, s. 1 (2).
[6] See above, p. 26.
[7] By 32 Hen. VIII. c. 32, this remedy

was extended to joint owners for lives
or years. See 8, 9 Will. III. c. 31:
3, 4 Anne c. 18, s. 2.
[8] 3, 4 Will. IV. c. 27, s. 36. As to
the effect of this Act upon the right to
partition, see judgment of North, J.,
in Mayfair Property Co. v. Johnston,
1894, 1 Ch. 508. See also Parker v.
Gerrard, Amb. 236.

Chancery was willing to redress an unequal partition[1]. Spence, probably in view of these cases, assigns to the reign of Elizabeth the beginning of the jurisdiction of Chancery in partition matters[2]. Mr Baildon, however, has found an instance in the first half of the fifteenth century. William and Thomas Brigge, brothers, were joint tenants under their father's will. The feoffee under the will divided the lands between the brothers, but Thomas occupied the whole "contrarie to lawe, conscience and the wille." The plaintiff, William, complained that no partition was made, "for the which particion to be made there is non accyon atte common lawe," saying that the partition thereof may not be had save through the gracious aid of the Bishop of Bath and Wells, Chancellor of England[3].

Partition by commission on a bill filed in Chancery prevailed over other methods, and was found to be convenient[4]. The confirmation by the Court of the Commissioners' certificates being only equitable, the legal title had to be given by mutual conveyances[5]. Jurisdiction in partition cases still belongs to the Chancery Courts[6], which have now under the Partition Acts[7] a power to order the sale of the property jointly held. In *Pemberton v. Barnes*, Lord Hatherley, L.C., thus summed up the law:—"The Court is at liberty at the request of a person holding one-tenth, and against the wish of the persons holding the other nine-tenths, to order a sale, if from the nature of the property, or from the number of the persons interested, the Court thinks it right and reasonable to do so. If the

[1] At p. 155. See the long editorial note to Co. Litt. 169 a: and Foster, *Joint Ownership and Partition of Real Estate*, Chapter X.

[2] *Equit. Jur.* I. 654.

[3] *Select Cases in Chancery* (Selden Society, 10), 136. It is not recorded that the plaintiff succeeded.

[4] See the Lord Chancellor's observations in Calmady v. Calmady, 2 Ves. Junr. 569. Chancery jurisdiction in enforcing partition between joint tenants or tenants in common did not apply to copyhold lands until the

Copyhold Act, 1841. See Jope v. Morshead, 6 Beav. 213: 4, 5 Vict. c. 35, s. 85: 57, 58 Vict. c. 46, s. 87.

[5] See Jenks, *Modern Land Law*, p. 352: Attorney-General, etc. v. Hamilton, etc. 1 Madd. 214: Hughes v. D'Arcy, Ir. Rep. 8 Eq. 71: 8, 9 Vict. c. 106, s. 3.

[6] See Judicature Act, 1873, s. 34, subs. 3.

[7] 31, 32 Vict. c. 40, s. 3: 39, 40 Vict. c. 17. And see Settled Land Act, 1882, 45, 46 Vict. c. 38, ss. 3, 20.

Court finds that the parties entitled to a moiety or upwards desire a sale, the Court must order it, unless some good reason is shown to the contrary, or unless the persons objecting to a sale offer to purchase the shares of the persons desiring it, in which case the Court has a discretion to authorise them to do so[1]."

A convenient and cheap means of partition was also made possible by the Inclosure Acts[2], and is now to be had from the Board of Agriculture. In respect of lands to be inclosed, the Board can compel partition at the request of any interested party. In respect of lands not about to be inclosed, it can inquire whether partition would be beneficial to the co-owners; if satisfied upon this point, it can order partition with the consent of co-owners representing two-thirds of the property. Further, under the Settled Land Acts, 1882–1890, a tenant for life enjoys certain powers of sale and partition[3].

The increasing opportunities thus given to a joint tenant to sever a joint estate even without the consent of his co-owners, are an important contribution to the difficult subject of the rights of joint tenants *inter se*. These rights will be more fully discussed in a subsequent chapter[4].

We now pass to that form of collective ownership known as tenancy in common.

---

[1] L.R. 6 Ch. App. at pp. 693–4. See Porter *v.* Lopes, 7 Ch. Div. 358: Richardson *v.* Feary, 39 Ch. Div. 45. In Pitt, etc. *v.* Jones, etc., 5 App. Cas. 651, a joint owner asking for an open sale was held not compellable to sell his property at a valuation.

[2] See 8, 9 Vict. c. 118, s. 90: 11, 12 Vict. c. 99, ss. 13, 14: 12, 13 Vict. c. 83, s. 7: 15, 16 Vict. c. 79, ss. 31, 32: 17, 18 Vict. c. 97, s. 5: 20, 21 Vict. c. 31, s. 7: 22, 23 Vict. c. 43, etc. As to the effect of an award thereunder upon the allottee's title, see Jacomb *v.* Turner, 1892, 1 Q.B. 47.

[3] See 52, 53 Vict. c. 30, s. 11.

[4] See below, Chapter VII.

CHAPTER V.

TENANTS IN COMMON.

"LITTLETON, having spoken of parceners, which are onely by descent, and of joyntenants, which are onely by purchase and by joint title," goes on to speak of "tenants in common, which may be by three meanes, viz. by purchase, by descent, or by prescription[1]."

Between parceners, says Coke, there is a threefold privity, viz. in estate, in person and in possession; between joint tenants a twofold privity, viz. in estate and in possession; while between tenants in common there is privity only in possession[2]. In other words, of the four unities which are present in cases of joint tenancy, only one unity (namely of possession) need occur in tenancy in common: there may be "entire disunion of interest, of title and of time." "For if there be two tenants in common of lands, one may hold his part in fee-simple, the other in tail or for life; so there is no necessary unity of interest. One may hold by descent, the other by purchase from *A*, the other by purchase from *B*, so that there is no unity of title. One's estate may have been vested fifty years ago, the other's but yesterday, so that there is no unity of time. The only unity is that of possession; and for this Littleton gives the true reason, because no man can certainly tell which part is his own[3]: otherwise even this would soon be destroyed[4]."

There is no benefit of survivorship in tenancy in common. It is true that this benefit may be expressly conferred; but

---

[1] Co. Litt. 188 b : Litt. s. 292.
[2] Co. Litt. 169 a.
[3] "Onely this property is common to them both, viz. that their occupation is individed, and neither of them knoweth his part in severall." Co. Litt. 189 a.
[4] Blackst. *Comm.* II. 191-2.

tenants in common with express benefit of survivorship are to be distinguished from joint tenants[1]. As survivorship does not occur, the incidents of dower[2] and curtesy[3] apply to land held by tenants in common by prescription, whereas in joint tenancy the right of survivorship makes prescription impossible[4].

Tenancy in common is nothing more than a grouping of two or more sole and several ownerships of an undivided property. "Joyntenants have one joint freehold; tenants in common have severall freeholds[5]." This fact explains the absence of survivorship. The law is disinclined to hold a group of tenants in common to be one person: their separability is emphasised by statute. For the purposes of the Inclosure Act of 1895, where an interest in land is vested in several persons as joint tenants, such persons are entitled to one vote only in respect of their joint interest; where several persons are so interested as tenants in common[6], "each tenant in common shall be deemed separately interested and entitled to vote as if he were tenant in severalty[7]." And under the Conveyancing Act of 1881, where provision is made for covenants for title to be implied in a conveyance, such covenants are implied "*with the persons jointly*, if more than one, to whom the conveyance is made *as joint tenants*, or *with each of the persons*, if more than one, to whom the conveyance is made *as tenants in common*[8]."

Their holdings being several, tenants in common cannot strictly make a joint lease of their estate: if they purport to do so, they are construed to lease their several respective parts[9]. If they lease jointly for a term of years, they might apparently sue jointly for the rent reserved: if rent was reserved separately to each, separate actions were necessary to recover it. Littleton drew a distinction in such actions between the cases of per-

---

[1] See Doe dem. Borwell *v.* Abey, 1 Maule and Sel. 428 : see the judgment in Haddelsey *v.* Adams, 22 Beav. at p. 275.

[2] See Sutton *v.* Rolfe, 3 Levinz 84.

[3] See Sterling *v.* Penlington, 14 Vin. Ab. 512.

[4] See Litt. s. 310, and Coke thereon.

[5] Co. Litt. 189 a : see Litt. s. 311 : Pullen *v.* Palmer, 3 Salk. 207.

[6] Or as co-parceners.

[7] 8, 9 Vict. c. 118, s. 19.

[8] 44, 45 Vict. c. 41, s. 7 (i).

[9] See Thompson *v.* Hakewill, 19 C.B.N.S. at p. 726.

sonalty and realty, with which we shall deal later[1]. One of two tenants in common may lease his share to the other, and may distrain for rent upon any part of the land[2]. Further, their holdings being several, tenants in common convey to one another not by release but by such instrument as would be necessary for the conveyance of an undivided estate[3].

Tenancy in common, we have seen, may arise by prescription[4]. It may also arise upon the severance of a joint tenancy[5] or of a co-parcenary[6] through alienation without partition. Tenancy in common may further be created by express limitation (either at common law or under the Statute of Uses) or by what is called "construction of law[7]." At common law a gift which *prima facie* in its premises seems to create a joint tenancy, may by express words in the *habendum* create a tenancy in common[8]. "If lands be given to two to have and to hold, *scil.* the one moity to the one and to his heires, and the other moity to the other and to his heires, they are tenants in common[9]." "And the reason is," adds Coke, "because they have severall freeholds and an occupation *pro indiviso*[10]." "The law," said Blackstone, "is apt in its constructions to favour joint-tenancy rather than tenancy in common; because the divisible services issuing from land (as rent, etc.) are not divided, nor the entire services (as fealty) multiplied by joint-tenancy, as they must necessarily be upon a tenancy in common[11]." But equity, as we have seen[12], inclined the other way and favoured tenancy in common. The principle is laid down by Arden, M.R., in *Morley v. Bird*[13]; a number of decisions has established the effect of particular words in deeds or wills[14].

---

[1] See Litt. s. 316 : Abbott, C.J., in Powis *v.* Smith, 5 B. and A. at p. 851 : see below, pp. 54–6.

[2] Snelgar *v.* Henston, Cro. Jac. 611.

[3] 2 Preston Abstr. 77.

[4] Litt. s. 310. See above, p. 50.

[5] See Litt. ss. 292, 294; above, p. 42.

[6] See Litt. s. 309 ; above, p. 25.

[7] See the discussion in Windham's Case ; 5 Rep. 7, at p. 8 a, resolutions 3 and 4.

[8] Co. Litt. 183 b.

[9] Litt. s. 298.

[10] Co. Litt. 190 b.

[11] *Comm.* II. 193 : see Dyer, 25 a, pl. 158, and notes thereto.

[12] See above, pp. 39–40.

[13] See Tudor's *Leading Cases in Real Property*, at pp. 256–6.

[14] See *ib.*, as to what words will give a joint tenancy by deed, p. 271, or by will, p. 274, and what will give a tenancy in common by deed, p. 281, or by will, p. 283.

4—2

A tenancy in common by "construction of law" arises where a gift is made to two persons not capable of taking in joint tenancy. For example, before the Bodies Corporate (Joint Tenancy) Act of 1899[1] was passed, a gift to a man and a corporation would have created a tenancy in common[2]. An old case, which is a classical authority upon the dual capacity of a man who is also a corporation sole[3], decided that "if lands be given to John Bishop of Norwich and his successors and to John Overall doctor of divinity and his heires, being one and the same person, he is tenant in common with himself[4]."

Tenancy in common is extinguished either—

(a) "by uniting all the titles and interests in one tenant by purchase or otherwise, which brings the whole to one severalty": or

(b) "by making partition between the several tenants in common, which gives them all respective severalties[5]."

Voluntary partition could formerly be obtained by division and livery of seisin. For the partition of incorporeal hereditaments a deed was necessary, and is now required in all cases[6]. In compulsory partition tenants in common resembled joint tenants. They were not considered compellable at common law[7], although a case in 1202 shows a claim for partition. "Adam Cisn' demands against Robert de Ashstead that he should permit the wood of Ashstead, which is common between them, to be partitioned, so that each of them may have his reasonable part therein as it falls to him[8]." If jurisdiction in partition claims of this kind had been universal, there would have been no need for the Statute of Henry VIII., which, as we have seen, gave to joint tenants and tenants in common the writ *de partitione facienda* which had formerly belonged only to co-parceners[9]. The subsequent treatment of tenants in

[1] 62, 63 Vict. c. 20, s. 1. See above, pp. 31–2.

[2] Litt. s. 297.

[3] See Professor Maitland in the *Law Quarterly Review*, 16, pp. 335–354, and 17, pp. 134–5: Carr, *Law of Corporations*, pp. 30–32.

[4] Litt. 190 a: Y.B. 13 Hen. VIII. 14.

[5] Blackst. *Comm.* II. 194.

[6] Co. Litt. 169 a : 29 Car. II. c. 3 : 8, 9 Vict. c. 106, s. 3.

[7] Blackst. *Comm.* II. 194.

[8] *Select Civil Pleas*, I. (Selden Society, 3) case 121.

[9] 31 Hen. VIII. c. 1: see above, p. 46. A co-parcener and the alienee

common in respect of compulsory partition has been the same
as that of joint tenants; in fact, "in suing out a writ of partition, the party never shows whether he is a tenant in common
or jointenant[1]." It remains only to note the courage with
which the Courts have ordered the division of apparently
indivisible things. "The law says," observed Lord Eldon in
Turner v. Morgan[2], "there is no inconvenience in the partition
of a house....The difficulty is no objection in this Court. That
is laid down in *Parker v. Gerard*[3] and appears more strongly in
Warner v. Baynes[4]." The last-named case concerned the partition of a cold bath, while in *Turner v. Morgan* the plaintiff,
on partition of a house, was allotted "the whole stack of
chimneys, all the fireplaces, the only staircase in the house
and all the conveniences in the yard." Such singular results
would, of course, ordinarily be avoided by agreement between
the parties, and since the Partition Acts by the remedy of
sale. In spite of the Partition Acts, however, the jurisdiction
under the Henrican statute survives. In *Mayfair Property
Company v. Johnston* a garden wall was partitioned lengthwise
by North, J.[5]

Tenancy in common occurs in connection with "cross remainders." "When lands are given, in undivided shares, to
two or more, for particular estates, so as that, upon the determination of the particular estates in any of those shares, they
remain over to the other grantees, and the reversioner or
remainderman is not let in till the determination of all the
particular estates, the grantees take their original shares as
tenants in common, and the remainders limited among them
on the failure of the particular estates are known by the
appellation of cross remainders. These remainders may be
raised both by deed and will: in deeds, when the limitations
are legal, they can only be created by express words, but in

wills they may be raised by implication[1]." The process of creating cross remainders has an intricate appearance, but is no longer so cumbrous as formerly. "No technical precise form of words is necessary[2]."

The possession of one tenant in common was formerly regarded as the possession of the others. As in the case of joint tenancy[3], however, the law has been altered by the Real Property Limitation Act of 1833[4].

For some purposes tenants in common sue jointly, according to Littleton who distinguishes between actions in personalty and in realty[5]. "The old law certainly was, that in all real actions tenants in common must sever, and that in personal actions they must join. In mixed actions they were to sever[6]." In the case of an indivisible chattel (a hawk, or a hound, to borrow Littleton's illustration), two tenants in common must sue jointly, " for otherwise they should be without remedie, for one of them cannot make his plaint in assise of the moietie of a hawke or of a horse, for the law will never suffer any man to demand anything against the order of nature or reason.... Also the law will never enforce a man to demand that which he cannot recover, and a man cannot recover the moytie of a hawke, horse or any other entire thing[7]."

In *Thompson v. Hakewill* the Court held that where two tenants in common were entitled to the benefit of a covenant contained in a joint demise originally made by tenants in common, they must both join as plaintiffs in an action of covenant[8]. In *Coryton v. Lithebye* it had been said that "if two persons have an entire joint damage they may bring a joint action although their interests are several[9]." The *Tun-*

---

[1] Butler's note (82) to Co. Litt. 195 b. See 1 Preston *Est.* 96, 2 Preston *Abstr.* 78: Challis, *Real Property*, p. 339.

[2] Lord Kenyon, C.J., in Doe *v.* Wainewright, 5 T.R. at p. 431. See Elphinstone's *Introd. to Conveyancing*, pp. 403–4.

[3] See above, p. 34.

[4] 2 Cruise, *Dig.* 402: 3, 4 Will. IV.

c. 27, s. 12.

[5] Litt. s. 314–6.

[6] Littledale, J., in Doe dem. Poole *v.* Errington, 1 A. and E. at p. 755. See Curtis *v.* Bourn, 2 Mod. 61.

[7] Co. Litt. 197 : Litt. s. 314.

[8] 19 C.B.N.S. 713. See Foley *v.* Addenbrooke, 4 Q.B. 197.

[9] 2 Wms. Saund. 115.

bridge Wells Dippers' Case was decided on this principle.
"That case was, that of these dippers there were twelve in
number, all women, who were chosen by the freeholders of the
manor within which the wells lay, and approved of by the lord
of the manor; and that the business of a dipper was to attend
the wells, and deliver the water to the company who resorted
there, and the employment was attended with profits which
arose merely from the voluntary contributions of the company;
and the defendant having acted as a dipper without a proper
appointment, the dippers joined in an action against her for
the disturbance, which was thought by the Court to be well
brought, because although the dippers were severally entitled
to receive for their own several use such voluntary gratuities
as the Company were pleased to give them respectively, yet
with regard to a stranger's disturbing them in their employment, they were all jointly concerned in point of interest; and
that was a hurt done to all[1]."

In the *Winterstoke Hundred's Case*, where two joint owners
of a sum of money were robbed by offenders unknown, it was
decided that the two might join in an action upon the statute
of Winton; "otherwise it would be, if the sums were several,
and several properties[2]." It was held in *Cutting v. Derby* that
"where one certain injury is done to both tenants in common,
they shall have one certain remedy. But when the injury is
separate they may have several actions. One tenant in common
may bring an ejectment for his moiety[3], and make himself
tenant in common with the lessee of the other[4]." "It is true
that that case does not go the length of saying that the
tenants in common *must* sever, only that they may; but it
shows clearly that they have several interests in their share
of the damages[5]." Parties could not join in an action for
damages unless the damages, when recovered, would accrue to
them jointly; and accordingly tenants in common could not
sue jointly for double value for holding over, where there was

[1] 2 Wils. 423; cited in notes to
Coryton *v.* Lithebye at p. 116.
[2] Dyer, 370 a.
[3] Litt. s. 322: Co. Litt. 200 a.

[4] 2 Wm. Blackst. 1075.
[5] Tindal, C.J., in Wilkinson *v.* Hall,
1 Bing. N.S. at pp. 118–9.

no joint demise[1]. But after recovery on separate demises they
might sue jointly for mesne profits[2]. In an avowry for rent
they ought to sever, " because it goes to the realty[3]."

Since the removal of the distinction between real and
personal actions and the disappearance of pleas in abatement
the law has made special provisions applicable to cases of non-
joinder of parties[4]. In the present state of the law " it is clear
that one tenant in common can bring an action of tort without
joining the others[5]." As to contract, " where there is no express
contract with all, and their legal interest is several, the covenantees *must* sue separately; yet where the contract is entered
into with the covenantees jointly and the estate taken by
them is several, they *may*, at their option, sue jointly or
severally : jointly in respect of the joint contract, severally in
respect of the interest[6]." In *Roberts v. Holland,* an owner of
land, entitled to the benefit of a covenant running therewith,
devised his lands to six co-tenants. Wills, J., observed " they
are not seised *per mie et per tout,* but each has one undivided sixth part, and the covenant becomes equivalent to six
separate covenants, on which separate actions can be brought....
Where the co-tenants have separate interests, there are in effect
separate covenants[7].

" Where a mortgage is made by two tenants in common,
both of them must be parties to the action to redeem ; one
cannot redeem in the absence of the other....All the tenants
in common, or those who claim the equity of redemption under
them, are necessary parties to an action to redeem the charge
on the entirety[8]." It has sometimes been stated that where
the equity of redemption belongs to several persons as tenants
in common, one of them may redeem[9] (subject to an account

---

[1] See Wilkinson *v.* Hall, *ib.* 713.

[2] See Chamier *v.* Willett, 5 M. and
S. 64.

[3] Pullen *v.* Palmer, 3 Salk. 207.

[4] R.S.C., O. XVI. r. 11 : see above,
p. 35.

[5] Charles, J., in Roberts *v.* Holland,
1893, 1 Q.B. at p. 668.

[6] Platt on *Covenants,* p. 130.

[7] Roberts *v.* Holland, 1893, 1 Q.B.
at pp. 667–8.

[8] Chitty, J., in Bolton *v.* Salmon,
1891, 2 Ch. at p. 52.

[9] See Wynne *v.* Styan, 2 Phillips at
p. 306 : Waugh *v.* Land, Geo. Cooper's
Chanc. Cases, 129 ; where it is thought
the parties consented (see Fisher,
Mortgages, p. 689).

with his co-tenant). It seems, however, that one cannot redeem
merely his own share; for a mortgage must be redeemed entirely or not at all. Where two tenants in common mortgaged
an estate to secure a debt which they jointly and severally
covenanted to pay, and each of them attorned tenant to the
mortgagees of a part of the estate of which they were jointly
(as partners) in occupation, it was held that the mortgagees
could not by means of simultaneous distresses upon the goods
of each of the two, take goods which belonged to the two in
common[1].

Where a lease is deposited by two, and the bailee agrees to
keep it for the two, it is not in the power of one of the two
(or of assignees representing that one) to take it out of the
bailee's hands without the consent of the other[2]. Where four
co-owners pledged wine with a man, and the assignees of three
of the four offered to redeem, it was held that the refusal of
the pledgee to deliver the wine to the assignee would not
entitle the latter to maintain an action of trover[3].

It is competent to the assignees of a separate or distinct
portion of a patent to sue for an infringement of that part,
without joining one who has an interest in another part: the
damages recovered in such an action accrue to the former
alone[4]. It has further been held that the assignee of a patent
may maintain an action for an infringement, even though he
has acquired the right by assignment of two separate moieties,
and the party sued is the original grantee[5]. "One person
interested in a patent," said Malins, V.C., "is entitled to sue,
without making his co-owners parties to the action, either for
an injunction or for an account[6]." Similarly, one of several
co-owners of a name used as a trade-mark may on infringement
sue alone for an injunction and for the delivering up of articles
bearing the pirated mark, and for an account of the profits
made by the infringers, and for the payment of such part of

[1] Ex parte Parke. In re Potter, L.R. 18 Eq. 381.
[2] May v. Harvey, 13 East 197.
[3] Harper v. Godsell, L.R. 5 Q.B. 422.
[4] Dunnicliff and Bagley v. Mallet, 7 C.B.N.S. 209.
[5] Walton v. Lavater, 8 C.B.N.S. 162.
[6] Sheehan v. Great Eastern Railway Co., 16 Ch. D. at pp. 62–4.

such profits as he may be entitled to[1]. In a case of copyright, *Lauri v. Renad*[2], Kekewich, J., considered that, although the registered owners of a copyright take as tenants in common and not as joint tenants[3], yet any one or more of them may maintain an action against a stranger for an infringement of the entire copyright.

"Registered owners of a copyright," said Kekewich, J., "are tenants in common, and they are tenants in common of a peculiar kind. It is impossible for us English lawyers, dealing with the English language, to express our views except in the technical language of our law; but is not perhaps accurate even to call such owners tenants in common, and the Master of the Rolls (Sir George Jessel) took care not to call them simply tenants in common: he calls them 'tenants in common or part-owners,' and there are, or may be, many differences and distinctions between tenants in common and part owners, as regards their right *inter se*, and in respect of strangers[4]."

For these and other reasons we shall distinguish partnership from joint tenancy and tenancy in common, and shall discuss partners separately in the next chapter.

The wide question of the rights of other co-owners *inter se* will be considered in Chapter VII.

[1] Dent *v.* Turpin, 2 Johns. and Hemm. 139.
[2] 1892, 3 Ch. at p. 413.
[3] See Powell *v.* Head, 12 Ch. D. at p. 689.
[4] Kekewich, J., in Lauri *v.* Renad, 1892, at p. 413.

CHAPTER VI.

PARTNERS.

IT has been orthodox to describe partners as joint tenants who—by way of exceptional treatment—are denied the right of survivorship[1].

The value of partnership lies in the fact that it distributes risk and gives traders the capital and the opportunity to undertake enterprises beyond the scope of a sole trader. For commercial purposes men frequently become collective owners of property under conditions which at law constitute a joint tenancy. These men naturally desire to be able at their deaths to provide for their wives and children and to leave an established business to their heirs. If partners were treated wholly as joint tenants, the right of survivorship would leave the family of a dying partner penniless. In fact, the *jus accrescendi*, so valuable in cases of trusteeship[2], would be oppressive in cases of partnership. Consequently, when Coke comes to define the incidence of the right of survivorship, he says " an exception is to be made of two joynt merchants: for the wares, merchandizes, debts or duties, that they have as joynt merchants or parteners, shall not survive, but shall go to the executors of him that deceaseth; and this is *per legem mercatoriam*, which (as hath been said) is part of the lawes of this realm, for the advancement and continuance of commerce and trade, which is *pro bono publico*; for the rule is, that *jus accrescendi inter mercatores pro beneficio commercii locum non habet*[3]."

[1] See above, p. 41.
[2] See above, p. 36.
[3] Co. Litt. 182 a. See Fitzherbert, *N.B.* 117 E. How far the common law here adopts the *Lex Mercatoria*, is discussed in the judgment in Devaynes *v.* Noble, Sleech's Case, 1 Merivale, at p. 564. See also, in general, c. IX. of the treatise on the Law Merchant inserted in the 1900 reprint of the

Without this rule of the law merchant, trading partnerships would have been impracticable. At first the rule was asserted as a London custom[1]. In 1611 it was universal. "As Coke saith, there are four sorts of Merchants, that is Merchant Adventurers, Merchants Dormants, Merchants Travelling and Merchants Residents: and amongst them all there shall be no benefit by survivor[2]." It was applied to joint shopkeepers, "for they are merchants[3]." Gradually the rule was made to cover every kind of trader, all parties and manufacturers[4]. In so far as survivorship was a necessary element of joint tenancy, it was held that "in all cases of a joint undertaking or partnership, either in trade or any other dealing, the joint owners are to be considered as tenants in common[5]." For a time it was thought that the goodwill of the partners went to the survivor[6]; but modern cases decide otherwise[7]. The survivor may have the good-will through the circumstances of the case but not by the operation of law. He will not be allowed to appropriate to himself the good-will which belonged to the partnership[8], and "in case of necessity would be restrained by the Court, pending a sale of the good-will for the benefit of the partnership, from doing any act in excess of his rights which, if not stopped, would enable him to obtain the good-will or

Little Red Book of Bristol. For a comparison of the English and Roman Law of partnership, see Scrutton, *Roman Law and Law of England*, pp. 159–161.

[1] See Chamberlain of London's Case (33 Eliz.), 3 Leon. 264: Elwin *v.* Moor (37 Eliz.), Noy 55.

[2] Hamond *v.* Jethro; 2 Brownl. and Gold, 99.

[3] *Ib.*

[4] But not societies holding property as joint tenants not for gain. See Brown *v.* Dale, 9 Ch. D. 78 : Lindley, *Partnership* (1905, 7th Edn.), p. 381. See Jeffereys *v.* Small, 1683, 1 Vern. 217 (and see pp. 33, 360): Hall *v.* Huffam, 2 Lev. 188 : Martin *v.* Crompe, 1 Ld. Raym. 340: Crawshay *v.* Collins,

15 Ves. 227 : Elliot *v.* Brown, 3 Swanst. 489 : Lake *v.* Craddock, 3 Peere Williams 157 : R. *v.* Collector of Customs, 2 Maule and Selw. 223 : Dale *v.* Hamilton, 5 Hare, at pp. 384–5: Buckley *v.* Barber, 6 Exch. 164.

[5] Jekyll, M.R., in Lake *v.* Gibson; 1 Ab. Ca. Eq. 291.

[6] See Hammond *v.* Douglas (1800), 5 Vesey 539 : based perhaps on this decision, the case of Lewis *v.* Langdon, 7 Sim. 421, suggests that the right to use a firm's name might survive.

[7] See In re David and Matthews, 1899, 2 Ch. at p. 382 : Lindley on *Partnership*, pp. 381, 481-2.

[8] See Turner *v.* Major (a case, however, of special agreement), 3 Giff. 442 : Taylor *v.* Neate, 39 Ch. D. 538.

any part of it[1]." An attempt was made to enlarge the benefits
of a surviving partner by arguing that he had at least a *jus
disponendi*; but the Courts doubted if the survivor could, by
virtue of such a right, give a good legal title[2]. Surviving
partners hold as trustees for the representatives of a deceased
partner and are compellable to account[3].

What kind of co-owners, then, can partners be called?
Are they joint tenants? No: for they have no survivorship,
and are in that respect—as was said in *Lake v. Gibson*—"to
be considered as tenants in common[4]." Moreover in *Jackson
v. Jackson* it was held that a joint tenancy of two or more
persons is severed by their acting as merchants or partners[5].
But if partners cannot be called joint tenants, can they properly
be called tenants in common?

Between partnership and tenancy in common many differences exist[6]. If *A* and *B* are tenants in common, each has
a definite right to an equal half share in the undivided property: each can dispose of a moiety and nothing more[7]. But
if *A* and *B* are partners, each of them can, for partnership
purposes and in the partnership name, dispose of all the
partnership property[8]. Again, if *A* and *B* are tenants in
common, *A* can, without consulting *B*, transfer his interest to
X or *Y* so as to substitute a stranger for himself in the co-
tenancy. If *A* and *B* were partners, this could not be done[9].
Further, partnership involves community of profit and loss,
which is not necessarily a feature of tenancy in common. And
partnership is necessarily founded on a mutual agreement;
tenancy in common is not. Partnership contains important
elements of agency and trusteeship which are, as we shall see

[1] Romer, J., In re David and
Matthews, 1899.

[2] Buckley *v.* Barber, 6 Exch. 164,
181, etc.

[3] See Fitzherbert, *N.B.* 117 E :
Booth *v.* Parks, 1 Molloy's Ir. Ch.
Rep. 465 : Lake *v.* Craddock, 3 Peere
Williams 158: Partnership Act, 1890,
53, 54 Vict. c. 39, s. 20 (2).

[4] See above, p. 60, n. 5.

[5] 9 Ves. at p. 596.

[6] See Lindley on *Partnership*, pp.
26–7. Story, *Partnership*, ss. 88–100.

[7] See Co. Litt. 186 a.

[8] See Partnership Act, 1890, ss. 5–6 :
Lindley, pp. 145–8. See Barton *v.*
Williams, 5 B. and Ald. at p. 405.

[9] See Partnership Act, 1890, s. 24
(7) : Lindley, p. 396.

in the next chapter, largely foreign to tenancy in common.
One tenant in common had, apart from statute, no action of
account against the other unless (as Coke says) he had constituted him his bailiff[1]; but "if two Merchants occupy their
goods and merchandises in common unto their common profit,
one of them shall have an Action of Accompt against the other
in the County or in the Common Pleas[2]."

Partnership and tenancy in common also differ in relation
to partition. Tenants in common, as we have seen[3], might
have their land divided, but, until the Partition Acts, could
not be compelled to have it sold. "A partner has no right
to partition *in specie*, but is entitled, on a dissolution, to have
the partnership property, whether land or not, sold, and the
proceeds divided[4]." At the death of a tenant in common, his
real estate at law and in equity is treated as realty: but the
real estate of a deceased partner is treated at equity as personalty[5].

Lastly, though a tenant in common has no lien upon the
common property for outgoings[6], a partner has an equitable
lien (recognised by s. 39 of the Partnership Act of 1890)
upon partnership property for the debts of the firm and upon
any surplus assets for the obtaining of his share upon the
winding-up of the partnership.

All these points of difference show that, although co-owners
are sometimes also partners, co-owners are not necessarily
partners, nor partners necessarily co-owners. It therefore seems
preferable to describe partnership as a distinct form of collective
ownership rather than as an exceptional form of joint tenancy

[1] Co. Litt. 200 b : see below, p. 77.

[2] Fitzherbert, *N.B.* 117 D : this
action, however, was not much used
at common law. See Henderson *v.*
Eason, 17 Q.B. 701.

[3] Above, p. 52.

[4] Lindley, p. 27.

[5] Unless a contrary intention appears : see Partnership Act, 1890,
s. 22 : Lindley, p. 382 : Thornton *v.*
Dixon, 3 Bro. Ch. 199. The law is
fully discussed in the judgments of

North, J., in In re Wilson, Wilson *v.*
Holloway, 1893, 2 Ch. at p. 343, and
Davis *v.* Davis, 1844, 1 Ch. at p. 396.

[6] Except in the case of ships: a co-
owner of a ship has the right to
require the gross freight to be applied
first to pay the expense of outfitting
or repairing the ship for the voyage in
which the freight was earned. See
Green *v.* Briggs, 6 Hare 395, 408-9 :
Alexander *v.* Simms, 18 Beav. 80.

or of tenancy in common. For business purposes it is inevitable that one partner should be allowed to represent another and should stand in a fiduciary position towards him; this consideration prevents partnership from being co-ordinated with the forms of collective ownership which we have previously been discussing.

It was said in *Cox v. Hickman* that participation in profits is not conclusive evidence of the existence of partnership. Agency gives the test. A man is, or is not, liable as a partner, according as the trade has, or has not, been carried on by persons acting on his behalf[1]. Thus the question whether a partnership does or does not exist, is determined by considering the agreement between the parties and by gathering their intention from the facts of the case. This principle, affirmed in *Cox v. Hickman*, remains unaltered, although the second section of the Partnership Act of 1890 codified certain express rules for deciding whether a partnership exists or not.

The same men may be tenants in common of land and partners in business. If real estate be conveyed to two partners for the partnership account, they may become tenants in common of it; and they can convey only their moieties[2]. " It is not the law that partners in business, who are the owners of the property by which the business is carried on, are necessarily partners as regards that property. That conclusion is indeed expressly negatived by subs. 1 of s. 2 of the Act of 1890, and there are many cases before the Act to the same effect. There is the well-known case *Fromont v. Coupland*[3], in which two persons horsed a coach, and shared the profits derived from running it, and were held to be partners, though they were not partners in the horses by which the work was done. Take again the well-known case of ships used in common. Again, there is the case of *Steward v. Blakeway*[4], in which land belonging to co-owners as tenants in common was used for the

[1] Cox *v.* Hickman, 8 H.L.C. at pp. 304, 306, 312.

[2] See Balmain *v.* Shore, 9 Ves. 500: Thornton *v.* Dixon, 3 Brown, *Chanc.*

Cases, 199.

[3] 2 Bing. 170.

[4] L.R. 4 Ch. 603.

purpose of carrying on a quarrying business, but that of itself was not considered sufficient to make the co-owners partners in the land[1]."

It is thus possible for the co-owners of a mine to work it together for common profits, and to be partners in those profits but not partners in the mine. The anomalous results of such a position (in respect of all those points in which partners differ from co-tenants) are worked out in Lindley on *Partnership*[2], to which the reader is referred.

At common law one partner could not be prosecuted by another for stealing the partnership property[3]. The joint ownership was an answer to the criminal charge. But the Larceny Act of 1868 provided that if any person, being a member of any co-partnership, or being one of two or more beneficial owners of any property, shall steal or embezzle such property, every such person shall be liable to be convicted and punished for the same " as if such person had not been a member of such co-partnership or one of such beneficial owners[4]." The word " co-partnership " has been held not to include an association which is founded for mental improvement and not for the acquisition of gain[5]: but the Act was held to include a society which, consisting of thirty persons, had failed to register itself under s. 4 of the Companies Act of 1862[6].

With regard to civil proceedings, the Judicature Acts (with the Rules of the Supreme Court drawn up thereunder) have made a remarkable change. A partnership action at law is no longer defeated on the ground that the remedy lay in equity ; and no action can now be defeated by reason of the misjoinder or nonjoinder of parties.

Before the Judicature Acts one party could not sue another at common law upon any matter involving the partnership

---

[1] North, J., in Davis v. Davis, 1893, 2 Ch. at p. 401. See, on the other hand, Waterer v. Waterer, L.R. 15 Eq. 402, which is commented on in the same judgment.

[2] At pp. 30–32.

[3] See Lindley, p. 497, note (a):

Archbold, *Criminal Pleading* (23rd Edn. 1905), pp. 443–4 : 1 Hale 513 : R. v. Streeter, 1900, 2 Q.B. at p. 604.

[4] 31, 32 Vict. c. 116, s. 1. See Archbold, pp. 432, 444.

[5] R. v. Robson, 16 Q.B.D. 137.

[6] R. v. Tankard, 1894, 1 Q.B. 548.

account[1]. The action of account which originally existed between two merchants by the *lex mercatoria* somehow fell into abeyance; the common law refused to deal with suits involving the taking of partnership accounts. But partners could sue one another at common law upon express covenants or upon matters independent of the partnership. Thus in *Brown v. Tapscott* it was said "an action would lie on a covenant in co-partnership articles by one partner to pay another a certain sum if the partnership assets should prove deficient[2]." In a similar case the Court considered a certain agreement between partners was collateral and independent, "the damage arising from any breach of it being solely to the plaintiff and in no way to be brought into the account of profit and loss": consequently an action would lie[3]. If two partners, *A* and *B*, agreed to provide £50 for partnership purposes, and if *A* advanced £50 on behalf of and at the request of *B*, *A* could recover that sum by action at law[4]. Where at the expiration of a partnership two partners struck a balance which was in favour of the plaintiff and which the defendant promised to pay, the plaintiff was allowed to sue in *assumpsit*[5]. In *Jackson v. Stopherd*, Bayley, J., said it was clear that one partner could not maintain an action against another on the partnership account till the accounts of the firm had been wound up, and the balance due from the partner to be sued to the partner making the claim was ascertained. "But by special bargain between them, a particular transaction may be separated from the winding up of the general concern, and when thus insulated is taken out of the general law of partnership, constituting between the partners a separate and independent debt, on putting an end to their joint concern[6]."

[1] See Lindley, pp. 297–299, 591, 597–600: Bullen and Leake, *Precedents* (6th Edn. 1905), p. 267.

[2] Parke, B., 6 M. and W. at p. 123: the plaintiff was there also held entitled to sue his partner on a special *assumpsit*.

[3] Bleech *v.* Balleras and others: 29 L.J.Q.B. 261.

[4] See Crowder, J., in French *v.* Styring, 2 C.B.N.S. at pp. 365–6: also Venning *v.* Leckie, 13 East 7: Coffee *v.* Brian, 3 Bing. 54.

[5] Foster *v.* Allanson, 2 T.R. 479: Wray *v.* Milestone, 5 M. and W. 21.

[6] 4 Tyrwhitt, at p. 333.

Actions such as these may still be brought in the King's Bench Division, subject to their being transferred to the Chancery side under Order XLIX.

Before the Judicature Acts there was also a difficulty in enforcing contracts made between a partnership and any of its members. The partnership is not a legal entity independent of its members; it differs from the corporation in that it is not a distinct legal *persona*: it is a mere aggregate of individuals. To use the terms of Roman law, the *societas* is nothing, the *socius* is everything. Consequently an action between the partner and the partnership would be barred by the fact that the partner would be both plaintiff and defendant[1]. In a case of Edward IV.'s reign, a bond given by the Mayor and Commonalty of Newcastle to the then Mayor of Newcastle was held void on the ground that a man cannot be bound to himself[2]. As the theory of the corporation was developed, it was recognised that in such a case the Mayor and Commonalty, being a corporation, had a legal existence distinct from that of its members: thus in later years the man who happened temporarily to be Mayor might have been allowed to sue the Corporation. This development of a distinct legal entity did not occur in the case of a partnership: hence the partner and the firm could not sue one another[3]: the interposition of trustees was therefore necessary to provide machinery for enforcing contracts made between a partner and his firm[4]. Nor could two firms sue one another if they contained a member common to both[5]. Further, even at equity, it was generally necessary in any partnership dispute to have all the partners before the Court.

Thus, although in certain instances partners and firms

[1] See Bullen and Leake, p. 744: Lindley, p. 498.

[2] Y.B. 21 Ed. IV. ff. 15, 68: see Pollock and Maitland, *History of English Law*, I. 492.

[3] See De Tastet v. Shaw, 1 B. and Ald. 664; and the pleas in Worrall v. Grayson, 1 M. and W. 166, Gregory v.

Hartnall, *ib.* 183.

[4] See, for instance, Bedford v. Brutton, 1 Bing. N.C. 399.

[5] See Bosanquet v. Wray, 6 Taunt. 597. As to the possibility of a remedy in equity, see Piercy v. Fynney, L.R. 12 Eq. 69: Taylor v. Midland Rly Co., 8 H.L.C. 751.

could sue one another[1], there were serious difficulties at the common law before 1873. When, however, the Judicature Act was passed, these difficulties were removed. The fusion of law and equity makes it impossible for a plaintiff in the King's Bench Courts to lose his suit on the ground that his remedy lies in the Chancery Division. Actions involving partnership accounts are now entertained in the King's Bench Division[2], although liable (if complicated) to be transferred to the Chancery Division, to which the taking of accounts is assigned[3]. Further, the Rules of the Supreme Court now provide that "no cause or matter shall be defeated by reason of the misjoinder or non-joinder of parties[4]": they give wide powers of striking out and adding parties: and, "where there are numerous persons having the same interest," they allow one or more of such persons to sue or be sued on behalf of all[5]. Finally, it is now possible for a partnership to sue and be sued as a firm[6]. Thus a partnership gains a qualified and tardy recognition as a legal unit. It is still to be distinguished from a limited company, in that it has not a distinct legal *persona*, and in that the liability of its members is unlimited.

Partnerships therefore still lack some of the features of incorporated companies. Were England not content with her Companies Acts, she might well have imitated other countries[7] in creating a system of partnership with limited liability. Much was written before 1862 in favour of introducing such a system. Parliamentary enquiries were made, and Reports submitted, in 1837 and 1844[8]. Recently, in 1906, a Limited

---

[1] See the detailed list of actions possible and impossible between partners, in Lindley, pp. 593–600.

[2] See, for instance, York v. Stowers, 1883, W.N. 174: R.S.C. Order XV. r. 1.

[3] See Judicature Act, 1873, s. 34. See Leslie v. Clifford, 50 L.T. 590.

[4] Order XIV. r. 11.

[5] XVI. r. 9.

[6] XLVIII. r. 1.

[7] As to the Scotch system, see *Law Quarterly Review*, 10, pp. 342–3: as to Ireland, see the Anonymous Partnership Act (21, 22 Geo. III. c. 46). Compare the French *société en commandite*. See Carr, *General Principles of Law of Corporations*, pp. 111–3.

[8] A bill was drafted and submitted to the Parliamentary Committee of 1844, on Joint Stock Companies. See *Partnership en Commandite*, published anonymously in 1848.

Partnerships Bill was introduced, which passed through the
House of Lords. Much also was written before 1862 in favour
of giving legal recognition to the firm[1]. Though the incon-
veniences of joint traders have been largely remedied by the
passing of the Companies Acts and the Judicature Acts, some
of the old arguments still hold good. The separate personality
of the firm is now established by popular thought and mercantile
usage, if not by law.

The general position of partners is so fully and authorita-
tively treated in the many standard works on Partnership, that
it seems needless to deal further with the subject here. We
therefore pass on to consider the remedies possessed by co-
owners (other than partners) *inter se.*

[*Note.* Since the above was written, the Limited Partnerships
Act (7 Ed. VII. c. 24) has been passed. Under it there may be
general partners, liable for all debts of the firm, and limited
partners who are not liable beyond the amount of their contribution. The rules of equity and common law apply, except
where expressly modified by the Act.

The importance of the Act is doubtful. Conversely, in
1867, limited companies were allowed to have directors with
unlimited liability (30, 31 Vict. c. 131, ss. 4–8). This provision,
modelled like the Limited Partnerships Act upon French lines,
was little used.]

[1] See J. M. Ludlow, in the *Juridical Society's Proceedings* (1855), vol. II. p. 40 : and Cory, *Treatise on Accounts,* therein mentioned.

CHAPTER VII.

RIGHTS AND REMEDIES OF CO-OWNERS *INTER SE.*

PARTNERSHIP is pre-eminently a "living" form of co-owner-ship: it may almost be called the only form which contemplates the continuance of the relations between the co-owners. In all the other forms of collective ownership which we have discussed, it is plain that any complication must lead to disjunction. The history of these forms illustrates the tendency towards severalty.

In a consideration of the mutual relations between co-owners the analogy of the Roman Law is useful. Roman Law gave to co-owners the following remedies *inter se* :

(*a*) The right to partition[1]. If the property were physically divisible, it was so divided: if not, one co-owner took the whole and was obliged to compensate his fellows.

(*b*) The right to be indemnified for necessary expenses incurred on behalf of other co-owners.

(*c*) The right to damages if other co-owners in dealing with the common property did not show as much diligence as they would use to their own property.

These rights in Roman Law were based on obligations arising *quasi ex contractu*[2]. English Law, however, does not (except in special cases) place the relations of co-owners upon a foundation of contract or quasi-contract. Nor does English Law impose upon joint tenants or tenants in common a fiduciary character: unlike partners, they owe one another

---

[1] See Roby, *Roman Private Law*, II. 135.

[2] See Poste, *Gai Inst.*, 4th Edn.

pp. 386–7 : Sohm, *Inst.*, 2nd Edn. (Ledlie), pp. 428–9.

no special duty; they are not in general trustees for one another[1]: they are not agents for one another[2].

There is a striking passage in Littleton. Where there are co-owners of a horse, an ox or a cow, "if the one takes the whole to himselfe out of the possession of the other, the other hath no other remedy but to take this from him who hath done to him the wrong...when he can see his time[3]." Such statements of the law show the remedies of co-owners *inter se* to be, as Sir G. Jessel described them, "barbarous and antiquated[4]."

"Tenancy in common is an inconvenient kind of tenure; but if tenants in common disagree, there is always a remedy by a suit for a partition[5]," that is to say, by the ending of the co-ownership. Sometimes, as we have seen, the acts of the parties operate as a severance of the collective ownership; sometimes co-owners agree to divide the property; sometimes they can compel a partition. If an aggrieved co-owner does not wish to end the co-ownership, he has certain rights of action which vary according to the character of the co-ownership.

Of husband and wife, tenants by entireties, not much need be said. The wife counted for little in this form of co-tenancy, except for the fact that the husband could not convey the common property without her consent.

As to the mutual relations of parceners, the following dictum occurs in *Lord Mountjoy's Case*[6]. "Wray, C.J., said that he did agree to the case of two co-parceners, that one might let her moiety, yielding the moiety of the accustomable rent; for, in as much as they are in by act of law and of God, it would be hard that the frowardness of her co-parcener should prejudice her of the benefit of a fine which she might have by making of a lease of her moiety." The remedies formerly

[1] See Kennedy *v.* De Trafford, 1897, A.C. 180: In re Biss, Biss *v.* Biss, 1903, 2 Ch. at p. 57, where see at pp. 63-4, Romer, L.J.'s discussion of the old case of Palmer *v.* Young thereto appended.

[2] See Leigh *v.* Dickeson, 15 Q.B.D.

at p. 65.

[3] S. 323, where see Coke's commentary.

[4] Powell *v.* Head, 12 Ch. D. at p. 688.

[5] Cotton, L.J., in Leigh *v.* Dickeson 15 Q.B.D. at p. 67.

[6] Co. Rep. v. 5 b.

given to parceners *inter se* appear in Fitzherbert's *Natura Brevium* as follows:—

(i) They had the writ of Contribution. For example "if there be three or four co-parceners of lands and the eldest sister does the suit to the lord of whom the lands are holden and the others will not.allow her for her charges and losses according to the rate from the same suit, that co-parcener who did the suit shall have this writ of Contribution[1]."

(ii) They could not have the writ of *Mortdauncestor*, because it lay "against strangers and not against parties in blood[2]"; but they had the *Nuper obiit*[3]. For example, *A* demands against *B* a moiety of a messuage and of two hundred acres of land as his right and reasonable share which falls to him of the inheritance of *X* whose heirs they are and who lately died (*nuper obiit*)[4].

(iii) They had also the writ of right *de rationabili parte*[5]. These ancient writs were abolished in 1833[6].

In their respective relations *inter se* parceners, joint tenants and tenants in common are in the same position by reason of the unity of possession which is common to all of them. It is possible to group all these co-owners together in discussing their respective rights *inter se*: what is true of one will be true of another.

A. Remedies of co-owners of Land.

Before we deal with the rights and remedies of co-owners *inter se* in respect of land, some observations may be interposed on their rights in the title-deeds of land which is held in common. "Where two have an equal interest in a deed, and each may have occasion to use it......the only way of avoiding unseemly contest for the possession, is to rule that he who first

---

[1] F.N.B. 162 B.
[2] *Ib.* 196 L.
[3] *Ib.* 197 C.
[4] See Hakebeche *v.* Hakebeche, Y.B. 2 Ed. II. (Seld. Soc. 19), p. 97. For

other instances, see *ib.* p. 76, and Seld. Soc. 17, p. 90.
[5] F.N.B. 18 B.
[6] 3, 4 Will. IV. c. 27, s. 36.

has it may keep it; and this seems to be the result of the only authority which bears directly upon the subject[1]." A plaintiff, to recover title-deeds, would have to show a better right to the deeds than the defendant[2]; this is what a co-owner cannot do. "One co-parcener," says Viner, "may justify the detaining of the Charters of the land in coparcenary against the other in detinue, for they belong to her as well as to the other[3]." A co-owner's sole rights in the title-deeds of the common property are the rights (i) to hold them if he has them in his possession, and (ii) to inspect them, if they are not in his possession. "As between two persons, respectively admitting themselves to be tenants in common with each other, there is no doubt that the Court will order the production of title-deeds in the hands of either for the other's inspection[4]." Presumably the right to inspect implies the right to take copies[5].

With regard to the land itself, each of the co-owners "may enter and occupie in common the lands and tenements which they hold in common[6]." "If two have an estate in common for terme of years, etc., the one occupy all and put the other out of possession and occupation, he which is put out of occupation shall have against the other a writ of *ejectione firmae* of the moietie, etc.[7]" Upon this passage Coke comments thus:— "albeit one tenant in common take the whole profits, the other hath no remedie by law against him, for the taking of the whole profits is no ejectment; but if he drive out of the land any of the cattell of the other tenant in common, or not suffer him to enter or occupy the land, this is an ejectment or expulsion, whereupon he may have *ejectione firmae*, for the one moitie, and recover damages for the entrie, but not for the meane profits[8]."

[1] Jervis, C.J., in Foster v. Crabb, 12 C.B. at p. 150. See Brooke, *Abr.*, *Charters de Terre*; Y.B. 4 Hen. VII. f. 10. As to the survivorship of the deeds in cases of joint tenancy, see Lord Buckhurst's Case, 1 Rep. 2 a.

[2] See Yea v. Field, 2 T.R. 708.

[3] *Abr. Faits*, Aa 1: see Y.B. 3 Hen. VI. f. 19 b.

[4] Lord Eldon in Lambert v. Rogers, 2 Merivale, at p. 490: see Wright v. Robotham, 33 Ch. D. 106.

[5] See Bevan v. Webb, 1901, 2 Ch., Collins, L.J., at p. 74.

[6] Litt. s. 323.

[7] Litt. s. 322. See *Com. Dig. Estates* (K), 8.

[8] Co. Litt. 199 b.

The law was altered by the Statute of 4 Anne[1], and the decision in *Goodtitle v. Tombs*[2]. That decision established that if a tenant in common succeeded in a suit to recover his undivided share, he could maintain an action of trespass for mesne profits against his companion.

Ejectment might be maintained on an actual ouster; it followed that trespass (which in a sense is included in ejectment) would also lie[3]. It was not easy to say what circumstances would amount to ouster. In *Doe v. Prosser*[4], a sole and uninterrupted possession for thirty-six years by one tenant in common was held sufficient ground for a jury to presume that an actual ouster had occurred. On the other hand, in *Jacobs v. Seward*[5] it was held that the fact that one tenant in common put a lock upon the gate of a field held in common was not a sufficient ouster for a co-tenant to maintain trespass. It was there repeated that, unless there be an actual ouster of one tenant in common by another, trespass will not lie by the one against the other so far as the land is concerned[6]. Destruction of the common property might amount to ouster. For example, if there are tenants in common of a party-wall, "where there is a complete destruction by one tenant in common of that which he has in common with others, so that that other is wholly deprived of the use of it, an action of trespass will lie[7]." But a temporary removal of the wall "with a view to improve part of the property on one side at least, and perhaps on both, is not such a destruction as will justify an action of trespass[8]." In *Cubitt v. Porter*, Bayley, J., said "One tenant in common has

[1] C. 3, s. 27. See below, p. 78.

[2] 3 Wils. 118.

[3] See Coltman, J., in Murray *v.* Hall, 7 C.B. at p. 454, to be contrasted with the language of old cases like Hambleden *v.* Hambleden, 3 Leon. 262.

[4] 1774. Cowp. 217.

[5] 1872. L.R. 5 H.L.C. 464.

[6] See Lord Hatherley, L.C., at p. 473 : Murray *v.* Hall, 7 C.B. 441.

[7] Holroyd, J., in Cubitt *v.* Porter, 8 B. and C. 257. Where one tenant in common sued another in trespass and alleged a destruction of, and expulsion from, the common property, the defendant was allowed to pay money into Court in respect of the damage done to the plaintiff's share : Cresswell *v.* Hedges, 1 H. and C. 421.

[8] Bayley, J., in Cubitt *v.* Porter, at p. 265. See the remarks of Crompton, J., in Stedman *v.* Smith, 8 El. and Bl. 1 : Standard Bank of B.S.A. *v.* Stokes, 26 W.R. 492. And see Wilkinson *v.* Haygarth, 12 Q.B. 837, where soil was dug up and carried away.

upon that which is the subject-matter of the tenancy in common laid bricks and heightened the wall. If that be done further than it ought to have been done, what is the remedy of the other party? He may remove it. That is the only remedy he can have." This course was taken by ˙the defendant in *Watson v. Gray*, where Fry, J., held that the plaintiff had excluded the defendant from the use of the top of the wall, and that therefore the plaintiff was not entitled to damages for the throwing down of the wall, or to an injunction[1].

An aggrieved co-owner has the further right to have a receiver appointed. At first, apparently, the Court refused to grant a receiver as between tenants in common except in gross cases of exclusion[2]. In *Street v. Anderton* an equitable tenant in common in possession was ordered to give security for payment of the proportion of rents due to his co-tenants, otherwise a receiver should be appointed[3]. Lord Northington at an earlier date had refused to appoint a receiver of an undivided moiety, putting this question: how could a receiver let, set or distrain, or take any step without the consent of the other co-tenant[4]? In *Sandford v. Ballard*, one of several equitable tenants in common applied against an equitable tenant in common in possession for a receiver and for the application of the rents according to the rights of the parties. The Court appointed a receiver as to the share of the plaintiffs only, there being no proof of exclusion[5]. Later, when there was evidence that the defendant had excluded the rest, the Court granted a receiver over the whole property[6]. Where one tenant in common gave tenants notice to pay their rents to him only and advertised the estate for sale, a motion by a co-tenant for a receiver against him was refused on the ground that such conduct did not amount to exclusion. " Exclusion is where one tenant in common receives the whole rent and excludes his com-

[1] 14 Ch. D. 192, where see the discussion of "party-wall."

[2] See Milbank *v.* Revett, 2 Meriv. 405, and note (i) to Street *v.* Anderton (1793), 4 Bro. C.C. 414.

[3] *Ib.*

[4] Willoughby *v.* Willoughby, cited in note to Calvert *v.* Adams (1773), 2 Dick. 478. See also *ib.* p. 800.

[5] 1861.   30 Beav. 109.

[6] 33 Beav. 40.

panion from the share due to him[1]." "I may observe," continued
Leach, V.C., in that case, "that, even in the case of an actual
exclusion of one tenant in common by another, I doubt whether
this Court would appoint a receiver. If it were an exclusion
which amounted to an ouster at law, the party complaining must
assert at law his legal title. If it were not such an exclusion,
this Court would compel the tenant in common in receipt of the
rents to account to his companion; but would not, I think, act
against his legal title to possession: and the reason is, because
the party complaining may at law relieve himself by the writ of
partition. It is upon this ground that this Court has constantly
refused to restrain a tenant in common from cutting timber, or
doing any other act not amounting to destruction. Where the
estate in common is equitable, the Court does interfere;
because it acts against the legal estate of the trustee only, who
is guilty of a breach of trust if he permits one equitable tenant
in common in any manner to prejudice the interest of the
other[2]."

Doubt was cast upon Sir John Leach's decision by the cases
of *Hargrave v. Hargrave*[3] and *Searle v. Smales*[4]. In the latter
case, Stuart, V.C., observed: "the jurisdiction of this Court to
appoint a receiver has for its object the preservation of property
pending litigation, in order that ultimately the rights of all
parties interested may be fairly adjusted. That principle, it is
obvious, must be applicable in the case of tenants in common as
well as in any other[5]." In *Porter v. Lopes*, Jessel, M.R., considered that under the Judicature Act, 1873, s. 25, subs. 8, the
Court had jurisdiction to appoint a receiver until trial of an
action for partition, where a co-owner was in occupation but had
not excluded his other co-owners[6]. The learned judge there
said he should appoint a receiver unless the co-owner in occupation elected to pay an occupation rent[7].

The Court will appoint a receiver for the protection of infant
co-tenants: where there were two infant co-tenants, the elder

[1] 1824. Tyson v. Fairclough, 2 Sim. and St. 142.

[2] *Ib.* at p. 144.

[3] 1846. 9 Beav. 549.

[4] 1855. 3 W.R. 437.

[5] *Ib.* at p. 438.

[6] 1877. 7 Ch. D. 358.

[7] *Ib.* at p. 359.

on attaining twenty-one years was allowed to apply for the payment of his share, the receivership being declared to endure until both infants came of age[1]. Adult co-tenants may be appointed receivers[2].

Where tenancy in common of lands is complicated by the carrying on of a trade—as in the case of a coal-mine—receivers are granted or refused according to the principles of partnership law. If there are twenty owners of the same mine, "if each is to have a set of miners going down the shaft to work his twentieth part, it would be impossible to continue working the mine....Therefore, where persons are concerned in such an interest in lands as a mining concern is, the Court will appoint a receiver, although they are tenants in common of it[3]."

Besides this valuable remedy of a receivership, there is the remedy of an injunction. In 1809 Lord Eldon, in the case of *Twort v. Twort*, remarked upon the novelty of this latter remedy between tenants in common[4]. The ground of the injunction in that case was the fact that one tenant in common was occupying tenant to another, and was committing waste by felling timber and ploughing ancient meadow[5]. The more usual ground for an injunction is the commission of destructive waste. "If one tenant in common is doing merely what any other owner of land might do, the other cannot have an injunction merely on the ground that he does not choose to do so; but if it amounts to destruction, the Court will interpose[6]." In *Hole v. Thomas*[7] an injunction was granted between two co-tenants to restrain the cutting of immature timber or of trees or underwood at unseasonable times. It was there repeated that one tenant in common has a right to enjoy as he pleases, but that malicious destruction would be ground for an injunction[8]. It is

[1] Smith v. Lyster, 4 Beav. 227.
[2] Ramsden v. Fairthrop, 1 New Rep. 389.
[3] Eldon, L.C., in Jefferys v. Smith, 1 J. and W. at pp. 302–3. See Roberts v. Eberhardt, Kay 148: Story v. Lord Windsor, 2 Atk. 630.
[4] 16 Ves. 128: see the hesitation in Goodwyn v. Spray (1786), 2 Dick. 667.

[5] See Moor 71: Martyn v. Knowllys, 8 T.R. 145.
[6] Eldon, L.C., in Twort v. Twort, 16 Ves. at p. 128.
[7] 7 Ves. 589.
[8] See also Arthur v. Lamb, 2 Dr. and Son 428: and Durham and Sunderland Rly Co. v. Wawn, 3 Beav. 119. An injunction will be granted

not destructive waste for a tenant in common of a coal-mine to
get coal if he does not appropriate to himself more than his
share[1]. There the co-tenant has his remedy not by injunction
but by inquiry and account. And, in *Smallman v. Onions*[2], an
injunction to restrain the felling of timber, after being refused
on the ground of the equal rights of tenants in common, was
granted when an affidavit stated that the defendant in
possession was insolvent and could not pay the plaintiffs their
shares of the money to be produced by the sale.

" As each party is entitled to enter upon the whole property,
there can be no claim by one tenant in common against another
for an occupation rent. As to cutting down trees, and the
other acts of waste, each tenant in common has a right to
exercise acts of ownership over the whole property, and no
charge can therefore be sustained in respect of such an act[3]."
If, however, one co-owner, by committing destructive waste,
gains advantage, he is liable to account to his companions for
the proportions thereof which are due to them[4]. We have just
seen that a co-owner who works a coal-mine must account to
his companions. But he is allowed, in taking such an account,
to deduct the costs of winning the coal[5].

After discussing the action of account between two joint
merchants, of which mention has already been made[6], Coke
continues:—"If there be two joyntenants or tenants in common
of lands, and the one make the other his baylife of his moiety,
he shall have an action of account against him as bailife[7]." But
no such action lay (at common law) unless the defendant had
been constituted bailiff[8]. The mere fact that one tenant in
common collects the whole rents, does not constitute him bailiff
to his co-owners. A tenant in common, it has been recently

after decree made in a partition suit :
see Bailey *v.* Hobson, L.R. 5 Ch.
App. 180.

[1] Job *v.* Potton, L.R. 20 Eq. 84 :
Re Mary Smith, L.R. 10 Ch. 79.

[2] 4 Bro. Ch. C. 621.

[3] Kindersley, V.C., in Griffies *v.*
Griffies, 8 L.T.N.S. 758.

[4] See Co. Litt. 200 b : Martyn *v.*

Knowllys, 8 T.R. 145 : Twort *v.* Twort,
16 Ves. 128. See, generally, Co. Litt.
200 a and b ; Stat. Westminster II.

[5] Bently *v.* Bates, 4 Y. and C. 182.
Job *v.* Potton, L.R. 20 Eq. 84 : see
order at p. 99.

[6] See above, p. 65.

[7] Co. Litt. 172 a.

[8] *Ib.* 200 b.

decided, cannot, by leaving the management of the common property to his co-tenant, impose upon him obligations of a fiduciary character[1].

A Statute of 4 Anne introduced the following change:— "Actions of account shall and may be brought by one joint tenant and tenant in common, his executors and administrators, against the other as bailiff for receiving more than comes to his just share or proportion, and against the executor and administrator of such joint tenant or tenant in common[2]." The statutory and the common-law remedies are to be distinguished "because a bailiff at common law is answerable not only for his actual receipts but for what he might have made of the lands without his wilful default, as is expressly held in Co. Litt. 172a, and in many other books; but by the plain words of the statute a tenant in common, when sued as a bailiff, is answerable only for so much as he has actually received more than his just share and proportion[3]." The statutory action is not one for money had and received to the use of another; consequently a defendant may show that the money was lost without his fault[4]. It must be noted that the statute applies only to joint tenants and tenants in common, not to parceners.

The statutory remedy was fully discussed in *Henderson v. Eason*[5]. It applies "where the tenant in common receives money or something else, where another person gives or pays it, which the co-tenants are entitled to simply by reason of their being tenants in common, and in proportion to their interests as such, and of which one receives and keeps more than his just share according to that proportion...[6]. There are obviously many cases in which a tenant in common may occupy and enjoy the land or other subject of tenancy in common solely, and have all the advantage to be derived from it, and yet it would be most unjust to make him pay anything. For instance if a dwelling-house, or barn, or room, is solely occupied by one

[1] Kennedy v. de Trafford, 1897, A.C. 180.
[2] 4 Anne c. 16, s. 27.
[3] Willes, C.J., in Wheeler v. Horne Willes' *Rep.* at p. 210.
[4] See Parke, B., in Thomas v. Thomas, 5 Ex. at p. 33.
[5] 17 Q.B. 701.
[6] 17 Q.B. 719.

tenant in common, without ousting the other, or a chattel is used by one co-tenant in common, nothing is received; and it would be most inequitable to hold that he thereby, by the simple fact of occupation or use, without any agreement, should be liable to pay a rent or anything in the nature of compensation to his co-tenants for that occupation or use to which to the full extent to which he had enjoyed it he had a perfect right. It appears impossible to hold that such a case could be within the statute: and an opinion to that effect was expressed by Lord Cottenham in *McMahon v. Burchell*[1]. Such cases are clearly out of the operation of the statute.

" Again, there are many cases where profits are made, and are actually taken, by one co-tenant, and yet it is impossible to say that he has received more than comes to his just share. For instance, one tenant employs his capital and industry in cultivating the whole of a piece of land, the subject of the tenancy, in a mode in which the money and labour expended greatly exceed the value of the rent or compensation for the mere occupation of the land: in raising hops, for example." If he lost by the speculation, he could not call on his co-owner for a moiety of the losses, is he to be accountable for profits? The risk, the profit and loss, are his own; and what is true of an uncertain crop of hops is also true with respect to all the produce of the land, " the *fructus industriales* which are raised by the capital and industry of the occupier, and would not exist without it." To take all this is not to take more than his just share : " he receives in truth the return for his own labour and capital, to which his co-tenant has no right."

" In the case before Lord North in Skinner[2], in which it is said that, if one of four tenants in common stock land and manage it, the rest shall have an account of the profits, but if a loss come, as of the sheep, they shall bear a part, it is evident, from the context, Lord North is speaking of a case where one tenant in common manages by the mutual agreement of all for their common benefit: for he gives it as an illustration of the rights of a part owner of a ship to an account when the voyage is undertaken by his consent, expressed or implied. Where the

---

[1] 2 Phillips 134.   [2] Anon. in Chancery, Skinner, 230.

natural produce of the land is augmented by the capital and
industry of the tenant,—grass, for instance, by manuring and
draining—and the tenant takes and sells it, or where, by feeding
it with his cattle, he makes a profit by it, the case seems to us
to be neither within the words or spirit of the Act[1]."

Co-owners may sometimes share in a benefit which primarily
accrues to one only of them. In *Clegg v. Clegg*, the owners
of adjacent estates were tenants in common of the coal-mines
beneath. Their lessee constructed a shaft which opened into
the separate property of one of the co-owners: a question arose
as to the rents derived from the use of the shaft. The Court
adopted the principle "that what is done by the tenant of two
persons who have a joint interest in property, with a view to
the benefit of both, although done on the property of one, does
not leave in that one any exclusive right to the use of it for his
own benefit, so as not to entitle the person who bore his share
of the burden to his share of the benefit of the use of the work
thus constructed, to whatever purpose of advantage it may be
used[2]."

If a tenant in common in possession were neither tenant
nor bailiff of his co-owners, nothing could have been recovered
from him at law; nor does the Statute of Anne apply. It has
however long been the practice of the Court of Chancery and
of the Chancery Division to direct certain inquiries as, for
example, in *Hill v. Hickin*[3], with regard to occupation rent
as in *Turner v. Morgan*[4], or with regard to expenditure on
improvements as in *Swan v. Swan*[5].

The principle on which the allowance for improvements is
made is stated by Cotton, L.J., in *Leigh v. Dickeson*[6], where the
remedies mentioned by Coke[7] and Fitzherbert[8] are considered.
"No remedy exists for money expended in repairs by one tenant

---

[1] Parke, B., at pp. 720–2. See
Jacobs *v.* Seward, L.R. 5 H. 2, 464;
and compare Caledonian Coal Company *v.* Seaham Colliery Company,
1901, A.C. 554.

[2] 3 Giff. at p. 335. See Carter *v.*
Horne, 1 *Abr. of Cases in Equity*, 7,
where the circumstances appear to

have imported fiduciary conditions.

[3] 1897. 2 Ch. 579.

[4] 8 Ves. 143.

[5] 8 Price 518.

[6] 15 Q.B.D. at p. 67.

[7] Co. Litt. 200.

[8] The writs of contribution and *de
reparatione facienda*.

in common, so long as the property is enjoyed in common[1]; but in a suit for partition it is usual to have an inquiry as to those expenses of which nothing could be recovered so long as the parties enjoyed their property in common; when it is desired to put an end to that state of things, it is then necessary to consider what has been expended in improvements or repairs; the property held in common has increased in value by the improvements and repairs; and whether the property is divided or sold by the decree of the Court, one party cannot take the increase in value, without making an allowance for what has been expended in order to obtain that increased value; in fact, the execution of the repairs and improvements is adopted and sanctioned by accepting the increased value. There is, therefore, a mode by which money expended by one tenant in common for repairs can be recovered, but the procedure is confined to suits for partition[2]."

"Where the property is sold the allowance is paid out of the proceeds of the whole property[3]. The principle laid down by Cotton, L.J., does not apply to occupation rent, and the question does not appear to have been discussed in any case. It is no doubt proper that where one of several co-owners is charged with an occupation rent he should not be allowed to take any part of the fund without paying what is charged against him; but on the other hand it does not seem right that the rent should be charged against a fund which does not belong to him. Suppose that an actual tenancy existed between one of the co-owners and the others, and an arrear of rent was due from him, I see no ground for saying that his co-owners would be entitled to have a charge on his share for those arrears. They may be entitled to insist that nothing should be paid to him personally until he has made good the arrears due from him; or, in other words, to have the arrears set off against what

---

[1] *Quaere,* how if the repairs amounted to salvage?

[2] Leigh *v.* Dickeson, 15 Q.B.D. at p. 67.

[3] See In re Jones, Farrington *v.* Forrester, 1893, 2 Ch. 461 (where Cotton, L.J., is followed and Teasdale *v.* Sanderson, 33 Beav. 534, explained): In re Cook's Mortgage, Lawledge *v.* Tyndale, 1896, 1 Ch. 923.

he personally would be entitled to receive; but this seems to me to be their whole right[1]."

In *Teasdale v. Sanderson*[2], where one tenant in common had been in occupation and another sued for partition and an account of rents, it was held that unless the former were charged with an occupation rent, he could have no allowance for the repairs and improvements which he had carried out upon the property. The accounts were to be reciprocal.

One tenant in common has no lien against the share of another for payments in respect of the estate. Where *A* and *B* were joint owners of a house, and *A* had laid out upon it monies which he had obtained from *B*, it was held that *B* has no lien upon the property for the amount. The facts did not show a partnership; the law did not infer a contract: " it was nothing more than a joint occupation, under a joint ownership of the property, and, in that point of view, the source from which any money laid out by either party was obtained is immaterial, and does not give the person from whom the money is derived any lien[3]."

In deciding a case where life insurance premiums had been paid by a part-owner, Fry, L.J., said: "With regard to payments made by a part-owner, it appears to me that, except by contract, such payments give no title to the person making them against the other part-owner or part-owners of a policy. That payments made by a mortgagor, who is in equity a part-owner with the mortgagee, create no lien as against the mortgagee, was determined by Lord Romilly, M.R., in the case of *Norris v. Caledonian Insurance Company*[4]." An argument was urged from the law of contribution; it was held, however, that there was insufficient authority to establish " any such general proposition as that the right to contribution creates any lien on the property in respect of which the expenditure has been made[5]."

[1] Stirling, J., in Hill *v.* Hickin, 1897, 2 Ch. at pp. 580–1.

[2] 33 Beav. 534.

[3] Lord Romilly, M.R., in Kay *v.* Johnston, 21 Beav. at p. 537.

[4] L.R. 8 Eq. 127.

[5] Fry, L.J., In re Leslie, Leslie *v.* French, 23 Ch.D. at pp. 563–4, where see the discussion of Swan *v.* Swan (8 Price 518) and Hamilton *v.* Denny (1 B. and B. 199).

In *Hill v. Hickin*[1] it was held that, upon a sale of the common property, a sum certified as due from a co-owner in possession could not be set off against a mortgagee of his share, although it might have been set off against the co-owner himself. In *Heckles v. Heckles*[2] it had been previously held that, where a tenant in common mortgages his share and receives more than his share of the rents, the right of his co-tenants to have such excess brought into Court on sale of the entirety takes priority of the mortgagee. The former case was that of a legal, the latter of an equitable mortgage. Stirling, L.J., who gave judgment in each case, expressed in *Hill v. Hickin* a doubt as to his decision in *Heckles v. Heckles*.

The mortgagee of the share of one tenant in common could maintain a bill for an account against the mortgagor and the other tenants in common[3]. As tenants in common (when not partners or trustees) do not stand in a fiduciary relation to each other, one of two mortgagors, tenants in common, is not debarred from buying for himself the undivided equity of redemption in the whole[4]. For the same reason, one of two lessees, tenants in common, appears not debarred from obtaining a renewal of the lease for his own benefit, if the old lease contains no covenant as to renewal[5].

The position of part-owners of land under the Settled Land Acts may here be mentioned. Under the Act of 1882[6] "if in any case there are two or more persons so entitled [*i.e.* for life] as tenants in common or as joint tenants or for other concurrent estates or interests, they together constitute the

---

[1] 1897. 2 Ch. 579.
[2] 1892. W.N. 188.
[3] Bentley *v.* Bates, 4 Y. and C. 182. As to whether a mortgagee of common property has constructive notice of the title, see Cavander *v.* Bulteel, L.R. 9 Ch. App. 79.
[4] Kennedy *v.* de Trafford, 1897, A.C. 180.
[5] In re Biss, Biss *v.* Biss, 1903, 2 Ch. 40. The position of trustees or partners is different. As Sir W. Grant

in Featherstonhaugh *v.* Fenwick said : " one partner cannot treat privately and behind the backs of his co-partners, for a lease of the premises where the joint trade is carried on, for his own individual benefit : if he does so treat, and obtains a lease in his own name, it is a trust for the partnership." 17 Ves. at p. 311. And see the judgments in Biss *v.* Biss, 1903, 2 Ch. pp. 56–64.
[6] 45, 46 Vict. c. 38, s. 2 (6).

tenant for life for the purposes of this Act." Under the Act of
1884, " the consent of one only of such persons is to be deemed
necessary to the exercise by the Trustees of the Settlement
or by any other person of any power conferred by the Settlement[1]."

While the mutual relations of partners are regulated by
statute as well as in general by elaborate agreements, the
mutual relations of other part-owners are left uncertain. It is
as though the law sought to discourage co-ownership by a policy
of non-interference, and to drive co-owners either into severance
or into detailed agreements. In the case of co-ownership of
chattels, to which we now come, the great remedy of partition
is seldom so practicable as in the case of land; consequently
definite agreements as to the conditions of common enjoyment
are the more valuable. "The ancient and inconvenient rules of
the common law," however, were modified by Equity, "especially
as regards ships[2]." The relations of part-owners of ships come
nearer to the sphere of partnership, and are more open to the
attendant influences of trusteeship and quasi-contract, than is
the case with part-owners of other chattels. The position of
co-owners of ships therefore requires separate consideration.

B. REMEDIES OF CO-OWNERS OF SHIPS.

" Of ships," wrote Lord Tenterden, "'which are built to
plough the sea and not to lie by the walls,' commercial nations
consider the actual employment as a matter not merely of
private advantage to their owners but of public benefit to the
State, and therefore have laid down certain positive rules in
order to favour this employment, and to prevent the obstinacy
of some of the part-owners from condemning the ship to rot

[1] 47, 48 Vict. c. 18, s. 6 (2). See
Cooper v. Belsey, 1899, 1 Ch. 639,
overruling In re Colling's Settled
Estates, 36 Ch. D. 516: but not where
the shares were separate; see Re

Osborne and Bright's Ltd., 1902, 1 Ch.
335.

[2] See Jessel, M.R., in Powell v.
Head, 12 Ch. D. at p. 689.

in idleness[1]." "It is the primary object of such engagements
that the vessel should be employed: and if the owners do not
agree, it would be a sacrifice of all interests, and of the first
object of commercial policy, that she should be detained to
perish in port. It is a condition of such partnership, therefore,
that the majority must prevail in deciding upon the course of
employment of the vessel[2]." This peculiar power of the majority
to employ the ship was in England qualified by measures to
protect the unwilling minority. " For this purpose it has been
the practice of the Court of Admiralty, from very remote times,
to take a stipulation from those who desire to send the ship on
a voyage, in a sum equal to the value of the shares of those
who disapprove of the adventure, either to bring back and
restore to them the ship, or to pay them the value of their
shares[3]." In 1680 " A part-owner of a ship sued the other
owners for his share of the freight of the ship which had
finished a voyage: but the other owners did set her out, and
the plaintiff would not join with the rest on setting her
out, or in the charge thereof; whereupon the other owners
complained thereupon in the Admiralty, and by order there,
the other owners gave security, if the ship perished in the
voyage, to make good to the plaintiff his share; and if she
returned, to restore his share, or to that effect. And in such
case by the Law Marine and Course of the Admiralty, the
plaintiff was to have no share of the freight. It was referred
to Sir Lionel Jenkins to certify the course of the Admiralty,
who certified accordingly: and that it was so in all places, and
otherwise there could be no navigation[4]."

---

[1] Abbott, *Merchant Shipping* (14th
Edn.), p. 117.

[2] *The Margaret*, 2 Hagg. Adm. at
p. 276.   Apparently the will of the
majority is more important than the
employment of the ship. The Court
would not interfere where a minority
wished to employ the vessel and offered
to give security. See *The Kent*, Lush.
495: *The Elizabeth and Jane*, 1 W.
Rob. 278.

[3] Abbott, *Merchant Shipping*, p.
118.   See Lord Stowell in *The Apollo*,
1 Hagg. Adm. at pp. 311–2.   Story
(*Partnership*, s. 431) discusses the
"doubtful advantage" of the English
law.

[4] Anon.   2 Cases in Chancery 36.
See Sir L. Jenkins' letter to the Lord
Chancellor, Wynne's *Life of Jenkins*,
II. 792.

It was the business of a dissentient co-owner to notify his dissent, and to apply for a warrant to arrest the ship. In *Strelly v. Winson*, where no such course was taken, and where two part-owners navigated the ship against the consent of the third, with the result that the ship was lost, the loss was held to fall equally upon all three. "Though one of the partners did not consent to the fitting out of the ship, yet he would have been entitled to one-third of the freight. *Qui sentit commodum sentire debet et onus*[1]." In *Barnardiston v. Chapman*, plaintiff was tenant in common of one moiety of a ship and defendants of the other moiety. The defendants forcibly took the ship out of the plaintiff's possession, secreted it from him, and changed its name: it afterwards came into the possession of a man who sent it to Antigua, where it was entirely lost. In the course of one of the hearings of this case it was held "that if one tenant in common destroy the said thing in common, the other tenant in common may bring trespass or trover against him; and therefore, in this case, if the defendants had burnt or destroyed the ship, this action would have been maintainable against them: that where one tenant in common doth not destroy the thing in common, but only take it out of the possession of the others and carries it away, there no action lies by the other tenant in common[2]." King, C.J., asked the jury "whether by the defendants' force the ship was actually taken from the plaintiff and secreted and carried out of his power to preserve the ship? and, a destruction happening in those circumstances, whether it should not be found to be a destruction by the defendants' means?" The jury found for the plaintiff with damages, and a new trial was refused[3].

In *Davis v. Johnston*[4] a dissentient part-owner, who had taken security for his share, was held not entitled to any share of the profits of the voyage, but was compelled to pay his proportion of the cost of outfit and repairs of the ship incurred up to the time of the arrest. It has been said that the law

---

[1] 1684. 1 Vern. 296. See Horn *v.* Gilpin, Amb. 255, where the report of Strelly *v.* Winson is corrected.

[2] See Holt, C.J., in Boson *v.* Sand-ford, Carth. 63 : Graves *v.* Sawcer, Sir T. Raymond, 15.

[3] See note in 4 East, at p. 121.

[4] 4 Sim. 539.

as to the earnings of a ship follows the general principles of partnership law[1]. A part-owner has the right to have the gross freight applied in paying the expenses of the refitting and outfit of the ship before any division amongst the part-owners shall be made. Similarly, expenses of repairing a ship's hull with a view to a particular adventure which could not otherwise have been undertaken (even if such expenditure were not exhausted with the adventure) are to be paid out of the gross freight before distribution[2]. Where the owner of seven-eighths of a ship mortgaged it, and the mortgagee took possession of it after its return from a voyage, claiming seven-eighths of the gross produce of the cargo, it was held that the expenses of the outfit and of the voyage had priority over his claim[3]. In *Doddington v. Hallet*[4] Lord Hardwicke went so far as to hold that each part-owner had a lien on the ship itself and on the proceeds of the sale of the ship for any sum due to him on an account between the part-owners. This view was adopted in America "as best founded in principle and public policy and convenience[5]"; but has not survived in England[6].

The jurisdiction of the Admiralty Court was thus stated in *Haly v. Goodson*[7] in 1816: "The Court of Admiralty is open all the year round to applications of this nature by part-owners of ships, and it has jurisdiction to take an account and to order security to be given on the footing of the respective shares, when the amount of those shares is apparent. But when the shares are unascertained, and their amount is in dispute, the Admiralty Court has no jurisdiction: the Court of Chancery will then interfere by injunction to restrain the sailing of the ship until the share of the dissentient part-owner be ascertained and security given to the amount of it."

By s. 8 of the Admiralty Court Act, 1861, it was provided

---

[1] See Green *v.* Briggs, 6 Hare at p. 406 : Lindsay *v.* Gibbs, 22 Beav. at p. 532.

[2] Green *v.* Briggs, 6 Hare 395.

[3] Alexander *v.* Simms, 18 Beav. 80.

[4] 1 Ves. Senr. 497.

[5] Story, *Partnership*, s. 444. See Green *v.* Briggs, 6 Hare at p. 401.

[6] See Green *v.* Briggs, 395 : Ex parte Young, 2 Ves. and B. 242 : Ex parte Harrison, 2 Rose 76 : *The Vindobala*, 13 P.D. 47.

[7] 2 Meriv. 77.

that "the High Court of Admiralty shall have jurisdiction
to decide all questions arising between the co-owners...of any
ship registered at any port in England or Wales, or any share
thereof, and...may direct the said ship or any share thereof to
be sold, and may make such order in the premises as to it shall
seem fit[1]."

In *The Hereward*, a minority of co-owners successfully
moved for the sale of the ship in an action for restraint where
the majority had formed a limited company to which they
transferred their shares[2]. The majority, said Bruce, J., "have
made it impossible that the ship can be profitably employed
in the general interest of the owners, unless the dissenting
owners, the minority of the owners, agree to come into the
company. In my opinion the managing owners of the ship,
the majority of the owners of the ship, have no right thus to
change the character of the ownership except with the consent
of all persons concerned."

The managing owner of a ship has otherwise wide powers.
He has authority " to conduct and manage on shore whatever
concerns the employment of the ship, and for that purpose has
authority to give orders for the necessary repair, fitting and
outfit of the vessel, in addition to seeing that she is properly
manned, properly sent to sea, and properly chartered for a
voyage." The liability of the co-owners is unaffected by the
fact that the ship is or is not insured[3].

The principles which govern the relations of part-owners
of ships are useful by analogy in the case of part-owners of
other chattels. These principles must however be disentangled
from the quasi-contractual principles of partnership by which
they are influenced, and from the provisions of various statutes
which have affected the registration of co-owners of ships.
Another class of co-ownership, in which also statute has required

[1] 24 Vict. c. 10, s. 8.

[2] 1895. P. 284. It was there said
that the Court ought to be very
cautious in directing a sale against
the majority of the owners. The
analogy of real property cases (see
Pitt *v.* Jones, 5 App. Cas. 651) was
discussed.

[3] *The Huntsman*, 1894, P. 214.

registration, may here be considered before we pass on to the
remedies of part-owners of chattels in general.

C. Remedies of Co-owners of Copyright and Patents.

In *Jeffereys v. Boosey* Lord St Leonards declared that copyright was one and indivisible, a right which might be transferred
but which could not be divided. "Nothing could be more absurd
or inconvenient than that this abstract right should be divided,
as if it were real property, into lots, and that one lot should be
sold to one man, and another lot to a different man[1]." Nevertheless, co-owners of copyright exist.

One part-owner of a copyright or playright cannot assign
the whole without the consent of his co-owners. If he purports
to grant a licence for performance without the concurrence
of his co-owners, the licence is invalid: it does not bind the
co-owners nor bar them from recovering their shares of the
statutory penalties which are imposed upon an infringer[2]. In
Lauri v. Renad Kekewich, J., allowed the assignee of three out
of four tenants in common of a copyright to sue a stranger for
infringement without joining the fourth co-owner as plaintiff[3].

Although it has been suggested—as in the case of copyright—that a right under a patent was indivisible, there may
be tenants in common of a patent[4]. And, where two persons
are thus tenants in common, and one dies, actions for infringe-
ments committed during the dead man's life survive to his
co-owner who can recover the whole damages[5].

In *Mathers v. Green* it was held that where a patent for an
invention is granted to two or more persons in the usual form,
each one may use the invention without the consent of the

---

[1] 1854. 4 H.L.C. at pp. 992-3. See
Pollock, C.B., at p. 940.

[2] Powell *v.* Head, 1879, 12 Ch. D.
686.

[3] 1892. 3 Ch. 402. Upon this point
the Court of Appeal expressed no
opinion.

[4] See Walton *v.* Lavater, 8 C.B.N.S.
162.

[5] Smith *v.* London and North
Western Railway Co., 1853, 2 E. and
B. 69. See National Society, etc. *v.*
Gibbs, 1899, 2 Ch. 289.

others; if he so uses it, he is not bound to account to the others for any share of the profits which he makes thereby[1]. Each of two assignees of a patent can work it without being liable to account for profits to the other: where one of the two is mortgagee of the other's moiety, the case is the same[2].

One of several co-owners of a patent can assign his share, and can sue alone for infringement[3]. There is some doubt, however, whether he should not account to another for money received from strangers for licences. "Suppose a patent is vested in two persons who are both using it, and a man infringes the patent, upon which they both complain, and a large sum of money is paid to one of them by the infringer to be allowed to make use of the patent, is it meant to be said that he can immediately release all the rights which the other person may have for the injury he has sustained by reason of the user of the patent? If such is the law," said Lord Romilly, M.R., "I must require some clear and distinct cases to be cited to me to establish what appears to me to be a violation of the fundamental principles of law, and contrary to natural justice[4]."

D. REMEDIES OF CO-OWNERS OF CHATTELS IN GENERAL.

The Judicature Act, 1873, s. 25, subs. 8, provided as follows:
"A mandamus or an injunction may be granted, or a receiver appointed, by an interlocutory order of the Court in all cases in which it shall appear to the Court to be just or convenient that such order should be made; and any such order may be made either unconditionally or upon such terms and conditions as the Court shall think just; and if an injunction is asked, either before or at or after the hearing of any cause or matter, to prevent any threatened or apprehended waste or trespass,

[1] L.R. 1 Ch. 29.

[2] Steers v. Rogers, 1893, A.C. 232. This settled the doubt raised in Hancock v. Bewley, Johns. 601.

[3] Sheehan v. Great Eastern Railway Co., 16 Ch. D. at p. 63; where Lindley on *Partnership* (7th Edn. p. 38), *q.v.*, is cited with approval. See Dent v. Turpin, 2 J. and H. 139; and above, p. 58.

[4] In re Horsley and Knighton's Patent, L.R. 8 Eq. at p. 477.

such injunction may be granted, if the Court shall think fit,
whether the person against whom such injunction is sought is,
or is not, in possession under any claim of title or otherwise,
or (if out of possession) does or does not claim a right to do
the act sought to be restrained under any colour of title; and
whether the estates claimed by both or by either of the parties
are legal or equitable."

It thus appears that co-owners of chattels in general may,
in cases of disagreement, have a remedy by way of injunction,
or receiver and sale.

We have already quoted the old common law doctrine of
Littleton that an aggrieved co-owner of a chattel "hath no
other remedie but to take this from him who hath done to him
the wrong...when he can see his time¹." There was also, as
Coke shows, a remedy against a co-owner who destroyed the
chattel. "If two tenants in common be of a dove-house, and
the one destroy the old doves, whereby the flight is wholly lost,
the other tenant in common shall have an action of trespasse...
for the whole flight is destroyed, and therefore he cannot in
bar plead tenancie in common. And so it is if two tenants
in common be of a parke, and one destroyeth all the deer, an
action of trespasse lieth. If two tenants in common be of land
and of mete stones *pro metis et bundis,* and the one take them
up and carrie them away, the other shall have an action of
trespasse *quare vi et armis* against him, in like manner as he
shall have for the destruction of the doves²."

"One joint-tenant or tenant in common or parcener cannot
bring trover against another, because the possession of one is
the possession of both³." "But if one joint-tenant, tenant in
common or parcener destroy the thing in common, the other
may bring trover⁴." An important judgment was delivered in
1872 by Lord Hatherley in the case of *Jacobs v. Seward⁵*. It
had been alleged that *A*, a co-tenant, entered upon fields held
in common with *B*, cut the grass growing thereon, made it into
hay and carried it off: *A* had also put a lock upon the gate of

¹ Litt. s. 323.   2 Wms. Saund. 111.
² Co. Litt. 200 a, b.   ⁴ *Ib.* 115.
³ Brown *v.* Hedges, 1 Salk. 290 :   ⁵ L.R. 5 H. of L. 464.

the fields, but it was not shown whether the gate was usually kept locked: moreover the Lord Chancellor passed over the locking as a necessary precaution against theft at haymaking time near London. *B* sued *A* in trespass, and also in trover for the destruction of the grass. It was clear that no action lay in trespass, unless there was an actual ouster of *B*; the facts were held not to justify an action in trespass. Nor did the claim in trover succeed.

"The question then is whether that making of hay by one tenant in common was in any way unlawful. The case of the whale, which was cited at the bar, is really a case expressly in point. That is the case of *Fennings v. Lord Grenville*[1]. The defendant there being a co-tenant in common of a whale, his servant turned all the whale's fat and blubber into oil, and appropriated them and the bone to himself, and the question was whether trover would lie in such a state of circumstances. That being the question between the parties, it was held that trover would not lie in that case, because the very purpose of capturing a whale was to turn it into oil. The co-tenant in common was therefore doing nothing that was illegitimate in the use that he was making of the whale....So long as a tenant in common is only exercising lawfully the rights he has as tenant in common, no action can lie against him by his co-tenant. Now it is perfectly lawful for a tenant in common to make hay, for somebody must make it, just as it is lawful for a tenant in common of a whale to make the blubber into oil. That is a perfectly legitimate purpose. It does not signify whether one or other of the tenants in common made use of it, it being made use of in an ordinary and legitimate way. No trover would, therefore, lie against the co-tenant in respect of his having done what he did.

"The cases in which trover would lie against a tenant in common are reducible to this. They are cases in which something has been done which has destroyed the common property, or where there has been a direct and positive exclusion of the co-tenant in common from the common property, he seeking to exercise his rights therein, and being denied the exercise of

[1] 1 Taunt. 241.

such rights. There was the case of a ship being taken possession of by one tenant in common and sent to sea without the consent of his co-tenant. In that case it was held that the property was destroyed by the act of one tenant in common, and there- fore trover would lie in respect of the co-tenant's share. But where the act done by the tenant in common is right in itself, and nothing is done which destroys the benefit of the other co-tenant in common in the property, there no action will lie, because he can follow that property as long as it is in existence and not destroyed. If it is sold, another question arises under the statute of Anne[1]."

" As regards the statute of Anne, that statute was intended to remedy a grievance which seems to have existed under the common law, namely, that inasmuch as trover would not lie, there appears, until the statute of Anne was passed, to have been great difficulty in a tenant in common getting his just rights with regard to that property which was his in common, but with respect to which he had not received his share. Accordingly the statute of Anne enacted that there should be an account, on behalf of one tenant in common against the other co-tenant in common, in respect of anything that he had received beyond his just share, and the remedy is there pointed out for taking that account[2]." The plaintiff's only remedy, therefore, in *Jacobs v. Seward* was by an action for an account under the statute.

Brooke's *Abridgement*[3] states that if two are jointly possessed of an ox, and one of them sells it entirely, an action of account will lie against the seller for a share of the money. Willes, C.J., agreed, because " it is a personal chattel," and because " by the sale and turning the thing into money the joint interest was gone: and I should think that not only an action of account, but even an action on the case for money had and received, might be well brought against him for it[4]."

In the case of ships, which has already been discussed, the

[1] *Ib.* at pp. 474–475. See 4 Anne c. 16, s. 27, and the citation from Henderson *v.* Eason, above, pp. 78–80.
[2] *Ib.* at p. 475.
[3] "Accompt," 20 ; based on Y.B. 47 Ed. III. Pl. 54.
[4] Wheeler *v.* Horne, Willes' *Rep.* at p. 209.

mere sale by one tenant in common was not regarded as a destruction of the common property[1]. In the case of other chattels "there may be such a dealing with the chattel by one of the joint owners short of its absolute destruction, as would amount in law to a conversion[2]." "The authorities seem to show that one partner or joint-tenant of a chattel cannot maintain trover against his co-tenant in consequence of his having taken upon himself to sell the subject-matter of the joint ownership....If, however, the thing be destroyed, or sold so as to change the property, as in market overt, the case is different[3]." "The true rule is, that the sale of a chattel by one of two joint-tenants is not a conversion, unless it operates altogether to deprive his companion of his property in it[4]."

In *Jones v. Brown* it was held that the secret removal of entire chattels by one tenant in common, without the consent or knowledge of the other, and for the purpose of selling them and applying the proceeds to his own use, does not amount to a conversion; further, that it is not an unlawful act for which the co-tenant can maintain an action at law, even though the removal has created a lien on the chattels by a third party[5].

In *Harper v. Godsell*, four joint owners of wine pledged the common property with the defendant, with a power of sale as security for repayment of an advance made by the defendant to them. When subsequently the interest of three of the four became vested in the plaintiff, the plaintiff tendered to the defendant the sum for which the wine was a security, and demanded the whole of the pledged property. In such circumstances it was held that the refusal of the defendant to deliver the wine to the plaintiff was not such a conversion as would entitle the plaintiff to maintain trover against the defendant. The wine had been sold under the power of sale, but not

---

[1] See above, pp. 86, 93: Barnardiston v. Chapman, 4 East 121: Heath v. Hubbard, 4 East 110.

[2] Coltman, J., in Mayhew v. Herrick, 7 C.B. at pp. 246–7.

[3] Cresswell, J., *ib.* at pp. 248–9.

[4] V. Williams, J., *ib.* at p. 250. See Barton v. Williams, 5 B. and Ald.

395. The contrary dictum of Parke, B., in Farrar v. Beswick, 1 M. and W. 682, seems wrongly reported; see 7 C.B. at p. 238. See generally 2 Wms. Saund. 114–116.

[5] 35 L.J. Exch. 345 : see Higgins v. Thomas, 8 Q.B. 908.

destroyed. Without the owner of the fourth part the plaintiff
was not in a position to demand the redemption so as to fix the
defendant with liability in trover. The owner of the fourth
part could himself have sold the wine without being liable in
trover to the plaintiff: under him the defendant had authority
to sell without being liable[1].

In the case of *Nyberg v. Handelaar*, the plaintiff, owner of
a gold enamel box, became joint owner with one Frankenheim
under an agreement that the plaintiff should have possession of
the box till it should be sold. He entrusted it to Frankenheim
for the purpose of its being taken to Christie's Auction Rooms
to be sold. Frankenheim, owing the defendant money, delivered
the box to him by way of security for his debt. It was held
that, under the agreement, the plaintiff had a special property
in the box which entitled him to possess it and to receive it
from the defendant[2]. "A joint owner of goods," said Lopes, L.J.,
"cannot maintain an action for the conversion of the goods
against his co-owner in respect of any act of the latter con-
sistent with his ownership. It follows that the plaintiff could
not, in the absence of any agreement as to the possession of the
box, have recovered it from the defendant[3]." But here there
was a special contract which modified the ordinary rights of
co-owners.

The law cannot undertake the impossible task of insisting
on equality of user between two collective owners[4]. Cases of
great difficulty must often arise. Suppose two men together
own shooting rights: may one of them shoot down the entire
game without rendering an account to the other[5]? May he
entertain shooting parties in such numbers as to destroy all the
game to the prejudice of his co-owner ? The comparative rarity
of decisions upon points of this kind arising between co-owners
may be due to the fact that the difficulties are usually anticipated
and prevented by detailed agreement, and further to the fact

---

[1] Harper *v.* Godsell, L.R. 5 Q.B. 422.
[2] 1892. 2 Q.B. 202.
[3] At pp. 205–6.
[4] See Caledonian Coal Co. *v.* Seaham

Colliery Co., 1901, A.C. 554.
[5] Presumably the decision in Fennings *v.* Grenville, 1 Taunt. 241, would
apply.

that an aggrieved co-owner has always, for what it is worth, the remedy of dissolving the co-ownership.

Nor has the law undertaken to divide equally between co-owners the profits arising from the common property. If two men together own a horse which earns profits on the race-course or in the stable, it cannot be supposed that one of the two would be allowed to keep the whole of such profits any more than he would be allowed to keep the whole of the interest on stocks and shares which were owned jointly. Where the profits, for example, of joint horse-owners, are accompanied by necessary expenses, there is usually (as in *French v. Styring*[1]) a special agreement between the co-owners. Such cases drift towards the doctrines of partnership, but are not necessarily cases of partnership[2].

"In all cases of such joint interests," wrote Story (with reference to "cases of account between tenants in common, between joint tenants, between partners, between part-owners of ships, and between owners of ships and the masters"), "where one party receives all the profits, he is bound to account to the other parties in interest for their respective shares, deducting the proper charges and expenses, whether he acts expressly by their authority as bailiff, or only by implication as manager without dissent *jure domini* over the property[3]." This view seems founded upon the cases of *Strelly v. Winson*[4], *Horn v. Gilpin*[5], and *Pulteney v. Warren*[6].

According to Story, the above-mentioned cases of joint interest "all involve peculiar agencies." This statement should be qualified by the recollection that the rules of agency do not apply to part-owners who are not partners. Where profits are obtained from property jointly owned, the facts alone will show whether the case is one of partnership[7], or whether an analogy

---

[1] 2 C.B.N.S. 357.

[2] See French *v.* Styring, *ib.*: Lyon *v.* Knowles etc., 3 B. and Sm. 556: Lindley on *Partnership*, pp. 26 etc.

[3] *Equity Jurisprudence*, I. s. 466. See Field *v.* Craig, 8 Allen, Massachusetts Rep. 357.

[4] 1 Vern. 297.

[5] Ambl. 255.

[6] 6 Ves. at p. 78.

[7] As to what is or is not partnership in such cases, see French *v.* Styring,

can be satisfactorily drawn from the rules which govern the part-owners of ships[1]. Absolute non-interference on the part of the law would allow a part-owner to snatch and hold all profits whether or not they resulted wholly or partly from his own efforts. Little though English law interferes between co-owners, such absolute non-interference could hardly be justified[2].

26 L.J.C.P. 181 : Lyon *v.* Knowles, 32 L.J.Q.B. 71: London Financial Association *v.* Kelk, 26 Ch. D. 107.

[1] See for example, Strelley *v.* Winson, 1 Vern. 297: Green *v.* Briggs, 6 Hare 325.

[2] On the whole of this subject of the remedies of co-owners *inter se*, see the valuable note (at pp. 32–8) in Lindley's *Partnership.*

CHAPTER VIII.

COMMUNITIES AS OWNERS.

COLLECTIVE ownership includes corporate ownership. Owner-ship by corporations (although, strictly speaking, it is outside the scope of this essay) deserves mention here because communal ownership often seemed likely to develop—and often did develop —into corporate ownership.

Definitions of "corporate" ownership demonstrate the vague and elastic use of the word "corporation." In the time of Henry VIII., Parliament, the "commune of the realm," was called a corporation[1]. In later days Sir Henry Maine spoke of the patriarchal family as a corporation[2]; one writer has included hundreds, counties and even parishes among corporations[3]. Not every *communa* or *communitas* was truly corporate[4]. The Jews were a *communa*[5], the *bacheleria Angliae* was a *communitas*[6], but neither of these was a corporation in the strict legal sense. By "corporation" is to be meant a body which is legally distinct from and independent of its individual members and even of the total of them, a body which is in law a separate person.

Not until the fourteenth century did this notion of corporate-ness appear in England, where it spread from the ecclesiastical

---

[1] Y.B. 14 Hen. VIII. f. 3.

[2] *Ancient Law* (6th Edn.), p. 184. See Pollock and Maitland, *Hist. of English Law*, II. pp. 244–5: Gierke, *Deutsche Genossenschaftsrecht*, I. s. 3.

[3] See Introd. by Miss Toulmin Smith to E.E.T.S. volume on *English Gilds*.

[4] See Pollock and Maitland, I. pp. 494–5.

[5] See *Select Pleas of the Crown* (Selden Soc. 1), p. 57 : *Select Pleas of the Jewish Exchequer* (Selden Soc. 15), pp. 121–2.

[6] See Pollock and Maitland, I. p. 495, n. 2.

to the common law, from chapter-house to borough[1]. It came in the guise of a foreign theory, imposing a fictitious singleness and separateness of personality upon the natural plurality of our native communities. It may be supposed to be shown established in our law by Coke's report of the *Sutton's Hospital Case*[2]. A corporation "may be *in abstracto*": "a corporation aggregate of many is invisible, immortal, and rests only in intendment and consideration of the law." Some think it is still an orthodox theory of corporateness in English law that the corporation should be considered a fictitious entity: some think otherwise[3]: some think our law has no scientific theory of the matter at all. Many English communities have not troubled whether to express themselves as neuter singular or as masculine plural. The first formal incorporation of towns five or six hundred years ago probably did little to alter their municipal management. London neither ceased to be a town nor lapsed into civic anarchy when a Stuart king revoked its charter of incorporation.

Naturally it is difficult to say when the corporation is first found in England in this exact sense. The authority of Dr Gross has easily sufficed to destroy the contention of Merewether and Stephens, who had placed the first instance of true civic corporateness in the reign of Henry VI.[4] The formula of municipal incorporation changed from time to time[5]: the thing itself existed in some form as early as the reign of Edward I. But whatever be the date at which our law was first conscious of its modern notion of corporateness, there must plainly have been plenty of pre-existing instances of communal ownership.

---

[1] See for the story of its development, Maitland, Introd. to Gierke's *Political Theories of the Middle Age*, p. xviii etc. : *Township and Borough*, p. 18 : *Domesday Book and Beyond*, pp. 353–4 : Carr, *General Principles of Law of Corporations*, cc. xi.–xii.

[2] 10 Rep. 32 b.

[3] See for the various views, Carr, *Corporations*.

[4] Merewether and Stephens, *Hist.*

of Boroughs, p.v. Gross, *Gild Merchant*, i. p. 93 : and *Bibliography of Municipal History*, p. xxvii : see Stubbs, *Const. Hist. of England*, iii. p. 586, and in the recent French edition by Prof. Petit-Dutaillis the editor's Appendix VIII. (i. p. 824) : Maitland, *Township and Borough*, pp. 18–20.

[5] See Maitland, Introd. to *Cambridge Borough Charters*.

Different writers seek the origin of ownership in systems of property-holding by the tribe, the clan, the village and the family in different sequences[1]. Though the social structures of India and Russia have been set side by side with those of Western Europe, the controversy which has raged round the "village community" has not yet subsided. Its progress may be followed through the pages of Maine and Seebohm, Von Maurer and Fustel de Coulanges, and in the more recent works of Mr Round and Professors Vinogradoff and Maitland. We do not propose to deal with it here[2]. The question whether property was first held by communities or by individuals recalls Aristotle's puzzle of the relative priority of owl and egg. Without committing ourselves to the hazardous position that all ownership can be traced back to an original communal system, we can be content to find in Domesday examples of common pasture and occasionally of co-ownership by geographical communities.

When Bracton and Azo came to write about ownership by the community (*universitas*), they found no better or more modern instances thereof than the *theatrum* and the *stadium*[3]. Amongst *res sacrae* they might have instanced the parish church, but they did not. (It is not suggested that the parish always owned its church,—indeed we know that the parson became a corporation solely for the purpose of such ownership[4]; but the idea was not impossible: the parishioners were concerned to repair the church[5].) And when Bracton and Azo speak of *res civitatis*, they do not consciously disentangle it from *res omnium civium*[6]: that is to say, they do not distinguish between

[1] See Maitland, *Township and Borough*, pp. 11, 20: *Domesday Book and Beyond*, pp. 340–1, 345: and see *L.Q.R.*, IX. pp. 36, 211 etc.

[2] See the valuable summary in Pollock, *Land Laws*, App. C.; and see Appendix I., on Les Origines du Manoir, in Prof. Petit-Dutaillis' edition of Stubbs' *Const. Hist. of England* (I. p. 765).

[3] Bracton and Azo (Selden Soc. 8).

[4] See Maitland, *L.Q.R.* p. 335: Co. Litt. 300 b.

[5] See *Select Pleas in the Manorial Court* (Selden Soc. 2), p. 150. Compare the case of the common mill: see Maitland, *Domesday Book and Beyond*, p. 144.

[6] See Gierke, *Deutsche Genossenschaftsrecht*, II. p. 211: Bracton and Azo (Selden Soc. 8), pp. 87, 90.

co-ownership and corporate ownership. Since a corporation, in the matured theory of our law, is an independent " person," it follows that " the corporators are not the owners, nor even the co-owners, of the corporate property[1]." A shareholder in a company incorporated for the purpose of keeping a strawberry-garden has no general privilege to enter and eat fruit; but one of two joint tenants of a strawberry-garden may be at liberty to do so. Theory has been obscured by practice to some extent. If shareholders can at any moment wind up a company and divide the profit, they tend to consider themselves co-owners according to the proportion of their several shares. Moreover, where members of a municipal corporation have had individual rights of pasture, the corporators are very like a group of co-owners. The Municipal Corporations Report showed that members of unreformed municipal corporations thought themselves entitled to do as they pleased with municipal property[2].

The distinction between corporate ownership and co-ownership, though modern, can be made to occur early. In 1293 the Prior of Dunstable sought to establish his right to land at Toddington, pleading that he was infeoffed by the men of the township. The answer of the defendants was that the feoffment was invalid, for some of them were not of age at its date[3]. That is to say, the men of the township held not in the capacity of a corporation but in that of co-owners. One may suspect the existence between these two capacities of a third, whereby townsmen could consider themselves to hold both jointly and corporately at the same time. Laymen's ideas were strong, and the mature legal theory of the lawyers was late in coming. It may be that this third capacity, or this fusion of the two capacities, corresponded with what Dr Gierke has told us of the *Genossenschaft*[4]. Significant of the uncertainty as to these two capacities and the difficulty of reconciling popular

---

[1] Markby, *Elements of Law*, s. 143.

[2] See Maitland, *Township and Borough*, Lecture I.

[3] See Pollock and Maitland, *H.E.L.*, I. pp. 630, 684.

[4] See Vinogradoff, *Growth of the Manor*, pp. 323–4: Gierke, *Deutsche Genossenschaftsrecht*, II. pp. 68 etc.: Heusler, *Inst. des deutschen Privatrechts*, I. p. 266: Maitland, *Domesday Book and Beyond*, pp. 341–2.

and scientific views is the fact that, when city and college were fully recognised as legal units, their official style was nevertheless plural: they continued to be " The Mayor, Aldermen and Burgesses of ——" and " The Master, Fellows and Scholars of ——." The case of Sutton's Hospital shows the law struggling to fit the singular nature of an institution to the plural nature of the men through whom it exercises its functions. Since institutions and offices, by reason of their perpetuity, had to be brought into line with municipal communities, corporations had to include not only the hospital but also the parson and the king.

Akin to the collective ownership of the early civic groups which ultimately became corporate, was the collective ownership of gilds which were sometimes non-corporate or quasi-corporate. Most gilds had charters (whether from the king or not): the Second Statute of Mortmain, which applied to lands purchased to the use of gilds and fraternities, drove gilds, like early boroughs, to seek charters[1]. Still a few unauthorised or "adulterine" gilds existed, as appears from the pages of Madox[2]. A form of community which was partly commercial and partly geographical gives another instance of quasi-corporate co-ownership. The London Adventurers who received wide territories and rights when they founded the plantation of Virginia, were in their first charter (in 1601) styled a Colony: it was not till their second charter in 1609 that they were made "one Body or Commonalty perpetual" to be " known called and incorporated by the name of the Treasurer and Company of Adventurers and Planters of the City of London for the First Colony in Virginia[3]."

Before we return to what are strictly geographical communities, mention may be made of the Inns of Court, whose members, though unincorporated, hold considerable property. Such non-corporate societies had always a difficulty in taking proceedings against one of their members for misappropriating the things co-owned. " One individual," it was said in a case

[1] 15 Ric. II. c. 5.

[2] See *Firma Burgi*, p. 26 etc.

[3] See Macdonald, *Select Charters illustrative of American History*, pp. 3, 12. In 1620 the Mayflower pilgrims, having no charter, adopted a quasi-corporate form by solemn mutual covenant. See *ib.* p. 33.

relating to the property of a lodge of Freemasons, "has as good a right to possess the property as any other, unless he can be affected by any agreement[1]." But, added the Lord Chancellor, "Supposing Mr Worseley's silver cup was taken away from the Middle Temple, the society must some way or other be permitted to sue." Until not long ago, a trade union or a friendly society could be robbed with impunity by its servants or agents because it had no representative of whom the law would take account[2]. For just the same reason in Booreman's case, in 1642, a barrister's suit against the Benchers of his Inn failed "because there is none in the Inn of Court to whom the writ can be directed, because it is no body corporate but only a voluntary society[3]." Nowadays the co-ownership of the property belonging to the Inns of Court brings us into the sphere of trusts, charitable or otherwise[4], which lies outside the scope of this essay. Nevertheless the trusts have not always been recognised or regarded. "It is matter of common knowledge that the buildings belonging to or occupied by some of the old Inns of Chancery have been dealt with as private property[5]."

When we mentioned geographical communities, we did not mean to imply that the boundaries of our villages were mapped out for the purposes of co-ownership. Boundaries were fixed in order to fix administrative responsibility, to ensure the catching of criminals, the payment of taxes and the like. And if villages are mentioned as collective owners, it is not implied that all villages were alike or that any village was conscious of the nature of its ownership. If fifteen men work fifteen strips of land as (*a*) corporators, or (*b*) joint owners, or (*c*) several owners, or (*d*) merely by some vague right of common user, they

---

[1] Lloyd *v.* Loaring, 6 Ves. at p. 776.

[2] See Ruegg and Cohen's *Present and Future of Trade Unions*, p. 4: Report of Royal Commission on Trade Disputes, 1906, *passim*. "The Act of 1871 was passed primarily with a view to preventing the treasurers and secretaries and officers of these societies from robbing them." Jessel, M.R., Rigby *v.* Connol, 14 Ch. D. at p. 489.

[3] March, 177.

[4] See the Clifford's Inn case, Smith *v.* Kerr, 1902, 1 Ch. 774. And compare Cunnack *v.* Edwards, 1896, 2 Ch. 679: In re Buck, Bruty *v.* Mackey, *ib.* 727. See also Fells *v.* Read, 3 Ves. 70 (the case of a society's tobacco-box).

[5] Cozens-Hardy, J., in Smith *v.* Kerr, 1902, 1 Ch. at pp. 522-3.

might not trouble themselves about the nature of their ownership so long as their rights of enjoyment were not infringed.
An early village would not concern itself with that power to
alienate which is now an important element of ownership[1].
Yet sometimes the point arose. Domesday has this interesting
entry:—*Hanc terram tenuerunt homines villae communiter et
vendere potuerunt*[2]: they held in common and could sell. There
seems no reason to suppose that this is an isolated case, though
we must remember Professor Maitland's warning that *homines
villae* may mean not *the* men of the vill but only men of the
vill. In 1296 there was a distinctly proprietary act by a village.
The village of Brightwaltham (*tota communitas villanorum de
Bristwalton*) appeared in Court and gave up its claim to a
wood in consideration of the fact that its lord gave up his claim
to another wood[3].

The claims of the lords remind us that we can scarcely say
that villagers collectively owned the soil. Even in the early
boroughs, whose development ran parallel with the process of
getting rid of mesne lords[4], there was no doubt as to who
owned the soil. Domesday Book suggests that at Cambridge
one Picot, the sheriff, had cribbed some of the *communis pastura*,
to build three mills thereon[5]. But the burgesses do not appear
to have complained in the capacity of owners; indeed in after
years the University declared "of the soil of Cambridge no
certain owner is known[6]."

The burgesses claimed to be their own lord. But although
the mesne lords might disappear, the burgesses had to reckon
with the king, from whom all privileges and charters flowed.

---

[1] See ante, p. 1.

[2] I. 213 b. See Maitland, *Domesday
Book and Beyond*, p. 143. Besides the
co-owning group knit together by neigh-
bourhood, Domesday Book also shows
us the co-owning group knit together
by relationship. See Maitland, *ib.*
p. 145.

[3] *Select Pleas in Manorial Courts*
(Selden Society, 11), p. 150. See

Vinogradoff, *Villainage in England*,
pp. 358–9 : see other examples of
group-action cited in his *Growth of the
Manor*, pp. 370–2.

[4] See Maitland, *Township and
Borough*, p. 71.

[5] D.B.I. 179 : *Township and Borough*,
App. s. 126.

[6] In 1616. *Township and Borough*,
pp. 10, 48 : Cooper, *Annals*, III. 110.

If in London the king took all escheats[1], this fact seems to show that the king still owned the soil. On a site of waste common land in Cambridge a certain Henry Eldcorn is said to have built a cottage hospital at some date *circa* 1200. The townsmen consented[2]; they got their municipal cottage hospital —such as it was—free. It is not recorded that the king was consulted. On the other hand, Barnwell Priory seems to have been built on a piece taken from the common by the express gift of Henry I.[3] Citizens who wished to be safe in approving their waste lands would doubtless have been wise enough to obtain special leave from the king[4]. In later days the University went directly to Queen Elizabeth for a lease of the common gaol of Cambridge[5].

Stuart persecution forced new charters upon unwilling towns. Consequently when the dynasty fell, and the pendulum swung back, the boroughs were not likely to hear much more of royal claims. But in early days the king's claim to the soil must have been strong. Escheats in boroughs were less important because burgage custom permitted the devise of houses by will. But whether they were valuable or not, the king probably never meant to abandon escheats, as the burgesses probably well knew[6].

If it is not unfair to take the right of escheat as a test of the ownership of the soil (and we must of course distinguish between *dominium* and *imperium*), it appears that the early boroughs cannot be said to have had collective ownership of their common lands. And if the boroughs had not collective ownership, the claim of the villages must be weaker still, for the villages were less completely organised and more exposed to seignorial influence. Yet since the ownership of the king

---

[1] Placit. Abbrev. 310. See *Township and Borough*, p. 71.

[2] See *Township and Borough*, App. s. 72. For other instances in which the community acted as collective owners of the waste, see Pollock and Maitland, *History of English Law*, i. p. 654.

[3] *Township and Borough*, App. s. 128.

[4] See *ib.* App. s. 125 : Pollock and Maitland, *History of English Law*, i. p. 653.

[5] But the gaol might be considered essentially Crown property. See Cooper, *Annals*, ii. 615 : *Township and Borough*, p. 90.

[6] *Township and Borough*, App. s. 116.

was vague and remote, the early geographical communities (if they thought about ownership at all) may have thought they held as collective owners,—*tenuerunt communiter et vendere potuerunt.*

Turning from the soil of the village to the soil of the whole country, we again meet the claims of the king. The Norman Conqueror, to confirm his conquest or to reward his followers, did not hesitate to distribute parcels of English soil. If in more democratic times men begin to ask whether the king owns the country or whether the country owns the king, the answer is that the king has been personified to hold the national land just as the parson was personified to hold church and glebe[1]. Various theories might have prevailed. "The greatest of artificial persons, politically speaking, is the State[2]": the State might have been treated as a corporation for the collective ownership of the country. According to an old report "the king and his subjects together compose the corporation, and he is incorporated with them and they with him, and he is the head and they are the members[3]." Had this notion been adopted, king and country would have been corporate in some fashion analogous to the groups of Dean and Chapter or Master and Fellows or Mayor and Burgesses. But this is not so. We may speak of "the country," "the public" and "the people," but it is the king, and not the mass of his subjects, who is owner of England[4]. No doubt popular thought will consider him trustee for the nation; Acts of Parliament may vest estates in him "to the use of the Publick[5]." The king, nevertheless, remains owner of England; like parson or dean he has two capacities, namely the one to take "to himself and his successors" and the other to take "to himself and his heirs[6]." He has property which is public and property which is private[7], just as the mayor of a borough may have in addition to his private

---

[1] See Maitland, *L.Q.R.*, xvi. 344.

[2] Pollock, *First Book of Juris-prudence*, p. 113.

[3] Plowden, 234, 261.

[4] See Salmond, *Jurisprudence*, p. 363.

[5] See 1 Geo. I. st. 2, c. 50 etc.

[6] Y.B. 13 Hen. VIII. 14.

[7] See statutory recognition of this fact in the Petitions of Right Act: see also the royal wills (*e.g.* Nicholas, *Royal Wills*, p. 59) and the Case of the Duchy of Lancaster, Plowden, 212, 223, 452.

property, official property such as seals, keys, weights, maces and books[1]. The difference between king and mayor lies in the fact that the latter is head of a corporation aggregate, while the former is a corporation complete in himself[2].

The sovereign (whether king or queen or whether described by the convenient title of "the Crown") thus legally personifies and represents England. But besides England there are the Colonies. If the Crown (by the British North America Act or the Commonwealth of Australia Act) permits Canada and Australia to deal with property and rights, and to sue and be sued, are Canada and Australia corporations? Or do they merely hold land which is really vested in the Crown? And if we import ideas of trusteeship, who are trustees and who are beneficiaries? From time to time the Australian Common-wealth and its constituent States, or the Dominion of Canada and its constituent provinces, have occasion to sue one another: the Crown and some of the governments of different parts of the Empire may become parties to an action *inter se.* Is then the Crown to be regarded as a legal unit which for certain purposes has become manifold? Or is the Crown a trustee for all parts of the Empire, even although their various interests may sometimes be in conflict[3]? In 1905 a member of the second contingent which New South Wales sent to the South African War, brought an action under a contract with the Government of New South Wales. The Lord Chancellor observed that it was not a matter of the obligation of the Colonial Government; "the Government in relation to this contract is the king himself[4]."

Are the Colonies legal persons? In 1876, in spite of the New Zealand Acts, James, L.J., said: "We must take notice that there is no such corporation as a Governor and Govern-

---

[1] See Miss Bateson's *Records of the Borough of Leicester*, III. pp. 3, 66-7.

[2] See Professor Hatschek, *Englisches Staatsrecht* (Tübingen, 1905), p. 93, for some consequences of the king, and not the State, being a corporation.

[3] See, upon this point, Maitland,

L.Q.R., XVII. 131: W. Harrison Moore, "The Crown as Corporation," *L.Q.R.*, XX. 351: Sir F. Pollock's note at p. 226 of his edition of Maine's *Ancient Law.*

[4] Williams *v.* Howarth, 1905, A.C. at p. 554

ment of New Zealand." Mellish, L.J., added: "It is said that
these New Zealand Acts have made the Governor a corporation
sole; but I have great doubt whether any Colonial Act could
make him a corporation sole[1]." If the Colonies are legal
persons, no doubt English law will call them corporate persons.
But if they have no personality except through the king, how
is one Colony to sue another?

Such questions as these may be idle enough, but they show
the absence of a straightforward method of dealing with land-
holding groups. The notion of corporateness has been so
developed in England as to disarrange the innate and necessary
communal ownership of land. The statutory incorporation of
Parish Councils and County Councils is a tardy recognition of
the rights of geographical communities; but it comes too late
to ensure to a community its natural collective ownership.
"The parishioners or inhabitants or *probi homines* of Dale are
not capable to purchase lands," said Coke[2]. "It is plain that
the inhabitants of a parish cannot claim title. They are not a
corporation[3]." And "persons, who without the sanction of the
legislature presume to act as a corporation, are guilty of a con-
tempt of the king, by usurping his prerogative....The usurpa-
tion is considered a criminal act....The acting as such a corporation, without charter from the Crown, is contrary to law[4]."

At the centre of all discussion about communal ownership in
England lies the fact that our law affects to see nothing but
unity in some co-owning groups, nothing but plurality in others.
For reasons which apart from history seem arbitrary, some
groups have become corporations and therefore privileged units:
others have not. The line between the two is difficult to draw.
Take the usual incidents of corporateness as described by
Blackstone[5]; most of them are found also to occur in the case

---

[1] Sloman v. Government of New Zealand, 1 C.P.D. at pp. 566–7. In this case the Crown and the Colony of New Zealand appear as parties to a contract. The Australian Common-wealth is by statute "to be deemed a corporation sole." See Common-wealth Acts, 1 Edw. VII. number 13 of 1901, 50 (1).

[2] Co. Litt. 3 a.

[3] Norwich Corporation v. Brown, 48 L.T. at p. 899.

[4] Duvergier v. Fellows, 5 Bingham. Best, C.J., at p. 216.

[5] *Commentaries*, I. 475.

of non-corporate bodies. An unincorporate body may have perpetual succession ; the Inns of Court are an example[1]. It may
have a common name, which (as in the case of a trade union) is
"the collective name for all the members[2]." It may sue or be
sued in that name, as we have already seen in the case of
partnerships[3]. It may deal with lands, sometimes more freely
than many corporations—for instance, than the religious corporations sole. It may have a common seal, as did the county of
Devon, which was not incorporated[4]. It may bind its members
by rules, as unincorporated clubs frequently do; in short, some
non-corporate bodies need envy corporations little. Although
a Lord Chancellor declared that it was the absolute duty of
Courts of Justice not to permit unincorporated persons "to affect
to treat themselves as a corporation upon the Record[5]," there is
nevertheless an established practice which permits a few members at equity to sue and be sued as representatives of an unincorporated body[6].

The law has occasionally administered identical treatment to
bodies corporate and unincorporate[7]. Although English law has
known "corporations by implication," we do not yet allow *de
facto* corporations to pass as corporations *de jure,* as is done in
the United States of America for many purposes[8]; but we do
appear more and more to be developing the personality of unincorporated groups, and such development must inevitably
bring them more into line with corporations[9]. It has been
observed that, as the Trade Union Act, 1871, created a legal

[1] Maitland, *English Law and the Renaissance*, pp. 26, 88.
[2] Lord Macnaghten, in the Taff Vale Case, 1901, A.C. at p. 440.
[3] See ante, p. 44.
[4] Pollock and Maitland, *History of English Law*, I. p. 535, n. 1: Russell v. Men of Devon, 2 T.R. 672.
[5] Lloyd v. Loaring, 6 Ves. at pp. 776-7.
[6] See Taff Vale Case, in *loc. cit.*, at p. 443: Meux v. Maltby, 2 Sw. 277.
[7] For instance (a) in respect of mortmain: see 23 Hen. VIII. c. 10 ;

(b) in respect of succession duties: see 48, 49 Vict. c. 51 ; (c) in respect of re-sponsibility for the acts of agents : see the Taff Vale Case, the principle of which is superficially affected by the recent Trades Disputes Bill.
[8] See Taylor, *Private Corporations*, s. 145: Gilfillan, C.J., in Finnegan v. Noerenberg, Prof. Jeremiah Smith's *Cases on Private Corporations* (Cambridge, U.S.A.), I. 150 (2nd Ed.) : Maitland, *Political Theories of the Middle Age* (Gierke), p. xxxviii.
[9] See above, pp. 67—8.

entity by the process of registration, "the legal entity, though not perhaps in the strict sense a corporation, is nevertheless a newly created corporate body created by statute distinct from the unincorporated trade union, consisting of many thousands of separate individuals, which no longer exists under any other name[1]." The gulf between the layman, who considers as a unit every group which acts as a unit, and the lawyer who grudges legal unity and legal entity to all groups except incorporated groups, is bridged in practice. As Lord Macnaghten observed in the *Taff Vale Case*, "a partnership firm, which is not a corporation nor, I suppose, a legal entity, may now be sued in the firm's name[2]." Groups which act as units cannot long be denied recognition as units.

Professor Dicey in his latest work[3] remarks that, "whenever men act in concert for a common purpose, they tend to create a body which, from no fiction of law but from the very nature of things, differs from the individuals of whom it is constituted." That, he says, is a fact which "has received far too little notice from English lawyers." Had that fact been recognised earlier, it must have exercised a remarkable influence upon the history and principles of collective ownership. The more it is recognised now, the truer will appear Professor Maitland's suggestion that it was a less extravagant fiction to call a corporate group a person than to call an unincorporate group no person[4].

---

[1] Lord Brampton in the Taff Vale Case (1901, A.C. at p. 442).

[2] 1901, A.C. at p. 440.

[3] *Law and Opinion in England,* p. 153.

[4] Maitland, *op. cit.*, p. xxxiv.

INDEX.

Account, action of, 65
  between joint merchants, 65, 77
  under 4 Anne, between man and wife, 13
  between joint tenants and tenants in common, 78–80, 93
  where co-owner is made bailiff, 77
  where co-owner of patent receives license-fees, 90
Account, joint, 40
  clause as to, 41
  joint banking, 38
Action for Partition, see Partition
Action of Account, see Account
of Ejectment, 72–3
Acts of Parliament, see Statutes
Admiralty, and co-owners of ships, 85, 87–8
Admittance of co-owners to copyholds, 34
Adulterine Gilds, 2, 102
Advowson, partition of, 27
  joint presentation to, 27
Agency, law of, and co-ownership, 61
  the test of partnership, 63
Agreement of joint tenants to sell, 37, 43
  to divide, 39
Alien as joint tenant, 32
Alienatio rei praefertur juri accrescendi, 44
Allowance to co-owner for improvements, 80–1
Ancestor, *persona* of, 18
Anonymous Partnership Act, 67
Application for partition under Inclosure Acts, 26, 48
Assignment of part of copyright, 89
Athens, co-heirs in, 20
Australia, Commonwealth of, 107–8

Bailiff, co-owner constituted, 77
  action against, under 4 Anne, 78
Bankruptcy, Trustees in, joint tenants, 30

Benchers of Inn of Court, 103
Bishop, as joint tenant, 31–2
  two capacities of, 31, 52
Board of Agriculture and Partition, 26, 48
Bodies Corporate Act, 32, 52
Body corporate, as joint tenant, 31–2, 52
Borough-english, 19–20
Boundary wall, 53
Bracton, on man and wife, 6–7
  on ownership by communities, 100

Canada, Dominion of, 107–8
Capacities, two, of bishop, 31, 52
  of king, 31, 106–7
Castles, partition of, 27
Certificate of Chancery Commissioners, 47
Chancery, jurisdiction in partition, 26, 46–8
  partnership actions assigned to, 66–7
Charitable trusts, 103
Chattels real, assignment of, by tenant by entireties, 11, 12
Church, whether owned by community, 100
Class, representation by one of a, 67
Club, action by joint owners, trustees of, 35
  rules of, 109
Coal mines, co-owners of, 76–7, 80
Co-heirs, 18–29
  see Co-parceners
Co-heirs, and the "united hand," 9
Collective owners, see Co-owners, Joint Owners
Colonists as co-owners, 102, 107–8
Colony and corporateness, 102, 107–8
Common law, larceny by co-owner at, 6, 64
  partition at, 25, 26, 45–6, 52
Commonwealth of Australia, 107–8

Communio bonorum, 5, 7
  in France, 5
  in Scotland, 10
Communities as owners, 98–110
  whether corporate or not, 98–9
  towns, 99, 101, 104–5
  villages, 100–106
  Bracton and Azo on, 100
  common church and mill, 100
  the *Genossenschaft*, 101
  gilds, 102
  colonies, 102, 107–8
  Inns of Court, 102–3
  Masonic lodge, 103
  trade unions, 103, 109–10
  England and Colonies, 106–8
  parishes, 108
  tend towards corporateness,108–110
Companies Act, 1862, 2, 3, 64, 67–8
Company, Virginia, 102
Compulsory Partition, by parceners, 26
  by joint tenants, 46–8
  by tenants in common, 52–3
Condominium plurium in solidum, 10–11
Conspiracy by man and wife, 17
Contract, co-ownership and, in Roman
  law, 69
  in English law, 69, 82
Contract, joint, parties to action on,
  35, 36
  to purchase in equal shares, 40
Contribution, writ of, 71, 82
Conversion, 94–5
Conveyance, by one co-owner to
  another, 45
  mutual on partition in Equity, 47
  see Cross Remainders, Joint Account Clause
Conveyancing Act, 1881, 41
Co-owners of patent, 57, 89–90
  of trademark, 57, 89–90
  of copyright, 57–8, 89–90
  of mine, 76–7, 80
  of ships, 79, 84–9, 93
  of land under Settled Land Acts,
  83–4
  rights and remedies of, inter se,
  69–97
    in Roman law, 69
    in English law, not *ex contractu*,
    69, 82
    no agency or trusteeship in, 69–
    70, 78
    by partition, 70
    in tenancy by entireties, 70
    in co-parcenary, 70–1
  in respect to land, 71–84
    right to title-deeds, 71–2
    right to enter and occupy, 72
    ejectione firmae, 72
    trespass and ouster, 73

Co-owners, *in respect to land*,
    party-walls, 73–4
    receivership, 74–6, 90–1
    rent, 74–5
    injunction, 76–7, 90–1
    destructive waste, 76–7
    occupation rent, 78, 80, 81–2
    action of account, 77–80
    inquiries as to occupation rent,
    80, 81–2
    inquiries as to allowance for im-
    provements and repairs, 80–1
    lien for payments to estate, 82
    for insurance premium, 82
    on mortgage and sale, 83
    one co-owner may secure whole
    equity of redemption, 83
    may obtain renewal of lease, 83
    as tenants for life under Settled
    Land Acts, 83–4
  in respect to ships, 84–9
    majority's power, 84–5
    minority indemnified, 85
    jurisdiction of Admiralty, 85,
    87–8
    incidence of loss, 86
    trespass, and destruction, 86
    partnership rules applied, 87, 88
    mortgage of, and lien, 87
    sale of ship, 88, 93–4
    majority of co-owners becoming
    limited company, 88
    powers of managing owner, 88
  in respect to copyright and patent,
    89–90
    assignment of part of copyright,
    89
    result of infringement, 89
    infringement of joint patent, 89
    assignment of part of patent, 90
    accounting for license-money, 90
  in respect of chattels generally,
    90–7
    mandamus, injunction or re-
    ceiver, 90–1
    common law remedy, 70, 91
    trespass, 91–3
    destruction of property, 91–3
    trover, 91–3
    exclusion, 92–3
    effect of sale by one co-owner,
    93–5
    conversion, 94–5
    redemption of property jointly
    pledged, 94–5
    rights modified by special con-
    tract, 95
    division of profits earned by joint
    property, 96
  See Communities as owners
Co-parcenary, by custom, 21–2

Co-parcenary, by common law, 22–3
  two kinds distinguished, 23
  course of descent in, 23
  how it arises, 24, 30, 49
  how it is dissolved, 25–6
  rarity of, 29
Co-parceners, 21–29
  escheat for felony, 21, 24
  as one heir, 23
  'seised jointly,' 24
  possession of one and all, 24
  not one person in law, 24
  no survivorship, 24
  can obtain partition, 24–6
  indivisible rights of, 27–8
  becoming tenants in common, 51
  rights of *inter se*, 70–1
   (*and see* Co-owners)
  right to title-deeds, 72
Co-partners, *see* Partners
Co-partnership, defined under Larceny
  Act, 64
Copy, right to, of title-deeds, 72
Copyhold, partition of, by parceners,
  25, 46, 52
  joint tenants of, 34
  surrender of, severs jointure, 44
  release by one joint tenant, 45
  Chancery and partition of, 47
Copyhold Act, 1841, 47
Copyright, survivorship and, 37
  infringement of co-owners', 57–8, 89
Corporateness, a royal concession, 2,
  99, 105, 108, 109
  early ideas of, 98–9
  incidents of, 108–9
Corporation, a distinct unit, 2, 66,
  98, 100–1
  ownership by, 2, 98, 100–1
  hostility of State to, 2
  husband and wife, 8–9
  as joint tenant, 31–2, 52
  different theories of the, 98–9
  early examples of municipal, 99
  parson, 100, 106
  king, 106–8
  de facto, 109
County, divisible, 28
  seal, 109
Covenant, action on joint, 35, 54, 56
Cross remainders, 53–4
Crown of England, indivisible, 28
  right of, in alien's moiety, 32
  represents country, 107–8
  see King
Curtesy, in parcenary, 24
  joint tenancy, 38
  tenancy in common, 50
Custom, of cities as to partition, 45
  of merchants, 41, 60
  parceners by, 21-2, 23

Damage, joint, 54–6
  infringing joint patent, 57, 89–90
Death, simultaneous, of joint tenants,
  35–6
De facto and *de jure* corporations, 109
De partitione facienda, 26, 46, 52
De rationabili parte, 71
Debts, estate of joint tenant not liable
  to, 38
Deed, required for partition, 25, 45, 52
Deed, mortgage, disclosure of trust
  in, 41
Demise, between joint tenants, 45
Descent, in co-parcenary, 22–3, 24–5
  no joint tenancy by, 30
  in tenancy in common, 49
Destruction of unities, 42, 51
  of common property, 73, 76, 91
  of ship, 86
Destructive waste, 76
Devise by joint tenant does not affect
  survivorship, 37
Dignities indivisible, 27–8
Disseisin, joint tenants after, 30
Dissolution of marriage, effect of on
  tenancy by entireties, 13
Distress, by one joint owner on
  another, 45
Dominion of Canada, 107–8
Dower, in parcenary, 24
  joint tenancy, 38
  tenancy in common, 50

Earldom, partition of, 27–8
Ecclesiastical Courts and movable
  things, 6
Ejectione firmae, 72
Ejectment, 72–3
Entireties, Tenancy by, 11–17
  see Tenancy by Entireties
  Tenants by, 11–17
  see Tenants by Entireties
Entry, by one joint owner, 34
  right of, 72
Equally, to hold, 14
Equitable jurisdiction in partition,
  26, 46–8
  remedies, as to severance of join-
  ture, 37, 43
Equity, hostile to joint tenancy, 39–40
Equity of redemption, one co-owner
  may secure whole, 83
Equity to a settlement, none in
  tenancy by entireties, 12
Escheat, gavelkind lands and, 21
  among common law parceners, 24
  in towns, 105
Estovers, indivisible, 27
Evidence, parol to rebut joint tenancy, 40
Exclusion, by co-owner, 74, 92–3
Executory trusts, 40

Extent, none upon estate in joint tenancy, 38

Family, the joint, 20
Father to the Bough, 21
Fealty indivisible, 27
  in joint tenancy, 51
Felony, forfeiture for, 32
  and see Escheat
Felo de se, 32
Feme sole, 15
Fiduciary, co-owners' relationship not, 69–70, 78, 83
Forfeiture for felony, 32
  and see Escheat
French partnerships imitated, 67–8
Fructus industriales, and action of account, 79

Gavelkind, in Wales, 21
  in Ireland, 21
  in Kent, 21–2
  descent in, incidents of, 21–2
  customs of, 22
Gemeinschaft zur gesammten Hand, 9
Genossenschaft, 101
Gift to man and wife and others, effect of, 13–6
Gilds, adulterine, 2, 102
  co-ownership by, 102
Goodwill, whether surviving in partnership, 60

Haereditas, 18
Hearthside child, 20, 21
Heir, parceners as one, 23
Heir-at-law, sisters as, *personae designatae*, 24–5
Heriot, joint tenants and, 34
Holding on, as joint tenants, 30
Homage, impartible, 27
Homeric family, 20
Honour, offices of, 27–8
House, partition of, 53
Husband and wife, *see* Man and wife

Ideal persons, 23
Improvements, allowance for, 80–1
Incidents, Blackstone's, of corporateness, 108–9
Inclosure Act, 1895, 50
Inclosure Acts, 26, 48
Indemnity, right to at Roman Law, 69
  of minority of ship owners, 85
Indivisible rights of parceners, 27–8
Infant co-owner, receiver appointed for, 76
Infringement of co-owners' patent, 57, 89, 90
  trademark, 57
  copyright, 58, 89, 90

Inheritance Act, 1833, and parceners, 23
Injunction against destruction, 74, 76–7
  under Judicature Act, 90–1
Inns of Court, as co-owning groups, 102–3
Inquiries in Chancery, 80
  as to occupation rent, 80, 82
  expenditure on improvements, 80–1
Insurance premiums, lien for, 82
Intention to sever jointure, 39–40, 44
Interest, unity of, 31, 32, 49
Ireland, gavelkind in, 21
  partnership in, 67

Joint account, money lent on, 40
Joint account clause, 40–1
Joint banking account, 38
Joint contract, parties to action on, 35, 56
Joint covenant, parties to action on, 35, 54, 56
Joint damage, action for, 54–6
Joint merchants, action of account, 65, 77
  no survivorship amongst, 41, 59
Joint mortgage, no survivorship in, 40–1
  redemption in, 56–7, 83
  set-off on sale of common property, 83
Joint owners, classes of
  tenants by entireties, 11–17
  parceners, 21–9
  joint tenants, 30–48
  tenants in common, 49–58
  partners, 59–68
  communities, 98–110
  of patent, 57, 89–90
  of trademark, 57, 89–90
  of copyright, 57–8, 89–90
  of mine, 76–7, 80
  remedies of *inter se*, *see* Co-owners
Joint tenancy, 30–48
  how arising, 30–1
  four unities in, 31–3, 42
  arising at different times, 32–3
  survivorship in, 35–8
  with several inheritances, 36–7
  exceptions to survivorship, 38–41
  equity hostile to, 39–40, 51
  severance of, 42–4
  favoured by law, 51
Joint tenants, 30–48
  becoming tenants by entireties, 13
  tenants by entireties becoming, 13
  bodies corporate as, 31–2, 52
  aliens as, 32
  consequence of four unities, 33–4

Joint tenants, entry of one and all, 34
  one tenant in copyhold, 34
  not a legal unit, 35
  survivorship, 35-8
  simultaneous death of, 35-6
  agreement to sell, 37-43
  partition by, 45-8
  becoming tenants in common, 51
  whether partners are, 59-61
  rights and remedies *inter se*, *see*
    Co-owners
Judgment debts and survivorship, 38
Judicature Acts, 64, 66, 67
Junior-right, 19-20
Jurisdiction of Chancery in partition,
    26, 46-8
  in partnership, 66-7
Jus accrescendi, among parceners, 24
  joint tenants, 35, 37-8, 44
  preferred to wills, 37, 44
    to burdens, 37
  alienatio rei preferred to, 44
  none among joint traders, 41, 59

Kent, gavelkind in, 21-2
King, and corporateness, 2, 99, 105,
    108
  as joint tenant, 31
  and escheats in towns, 105
  a corporation sole, 106-8
  owns and represents country, 106-8
King's Bench Division, partnership
    actions in, 66-7

Land, rights and remedies of co-owners
    inter se with regard to, 71-84
  and see Partition, Sale, etc.
Land Transfer Act, 1897, 18
Larceny, by partner, 64
  by wife, 13
Larceny Act, 1868, 64
Law Marine, 85
Law Merchant, 41, 59-60, 65
Lease, by joint tenant, whether
    severance, 42, 43
  by one joint tenant to another, 45
  joint, by tenants in common, 50
  by one tenant in common to
    another, 51
Legal and equitable mortgages, 83
Leicester, and primogeniture, 19
Lex mercatoria, *see* Law Merchant
Libel, publication to man and wife, 17
Lien, 62, 82
  in case of ships, 87
Life, joint estate for, 36
  tenant for, under Settled Land
    Acts, 83-4
Limited liability, 3, 68
Limited partnerships, 67, 68
Limited Partnerships Act, 68

Lord Great Chamberlain, office of, 28
Lot, partition by, in parcenary, 25

Man and wife, 4-17
  one person in law, 6, 13, 17
  as single owner, 7
  as owners with aliquot shares, 7
    without aliquot shares, 8
  no power of partition, 8
  a possible legal unit, 8
  tenants by entireties, 11-17
  effect of legal unity, 13-17
  joint gift to, effect of, 13-16
  joint banking account of, 38
  see Tenants by Entireties
Man and woman, gift to, afterwards
    intermarrying, 13, 37
Managing owner of ship, powers of, 88
Mandamus under Judicature Act, 90
Market overt, effect of sale by one
    co-owner in, 94
Marriage, and common property, 4, 5
  dissolution of, effect on tenancy
    by entireties, 13
  formerly severance of joint tenancy,
    43
Married woman, *see* Wife
Married Women's Property Act, 1882,
  effect of, on tenancy by entireties,
    15-17
  on criminal liability of wife, 13
  on severance of joint tenancy, 43
Merchant, Law, *see* Law Merchant
Merchants, the sorts of, 60
  trading to Virginia, 102
  customs of, 41, 60
  joint, no survivorship amongst, 41,
    59
  action of account, 65, 77
Mesne profits, recovery of, 26
  co-owners' right to, 72-3
Mill, common, 100
Mines, receivers appointed for, 76
  co-owners working, 76-7, 80
Misjoinder of parties, 35, 64
Moieties, of man and wife, 6, 11, 13, 33
  of aliens, 32
Money received for other co-owners,
    action by 4 Anne, 78-9
Moral persons, 23
Mortdauncestor, Writ of, 71
Mortgage, joint, no survivorship in,
    40-1
  redemption in, 56-7, 83
  set-off on sale of common property,
    83
  of ship, 87
Municipal ownership, 101
Mutual agreement, 101
Mutual agreement to sever joint
    tenancy, 43

Mutual wills, agreement to make, 44

Naturalisation Act, 1870, 32
New Zealand, 107–8
Non-joinder of parties, 35, 64
Nottingham, borough-english at, 19
Nuper obiit, 71

Occupation rent, payable by co-owner, 75, 77, 80, 81–2
Office found, 32
One person, man and wife, 6, 8–9, 13–17
  see Persona
Ouster, 73, 92
Ownership, definitions of, 1

Parage, 21
Parcenary, *see* Co-parcenary
Parceners, *see* Co-parceners
Parol agreement, partition by, in parcenary, 25
  evidence to rebut survivorship, 40
Parson, and layman as co-owners, 31
  incorporated, 31, 52, 100, 106
Parties, rules as to, 35, 64
  in joint action, 54–6
  in partnership actions, 66–7
Partition, in tenancy by entireties, 11
  in parcenary, 24, 25–6
    deed necessary, 25, 45, 52
    what rights of parceners are incapable of, 27–8
  in joint tenancy, 45–8
  at law and in Chancery, 45–8
  by commission, 47
  in tenancy in common, 52–3
  difficulty of, no objection, 53
  right to, in Roman Law, 69
Partition Acts, 26, 47, 53, 62
Partners, 59–68
  have no survivorship, 41–2, 59–61
  unlike joint tenants, 59–60
  unlike tenants in common, 61–3
  may also be tenants in common, 63–4, 76
  criminal liability of, 64
  suing one another, 64–5
  action of account, 65–6
  limited and general, 68
  see also Part-owners
Partnership,
  differs from tenancy in common, 62
  partition, 62
  lien, 62
  actions, 64–6
  accounts, 65
  can sue or be sued as a firm, 67, 109
  limited, 67–8
  rules applied to ship's earnings, 87
Partnership Act, 1890, 62, 63

Partnership articles, and survivorship, 41
Part-owners, 58
  of patent, 57, 89–90
  trademark, 57, 89–90
  copyright, 57–8, 89–90
  mine, 76–7, 80
  ships, 79, 84–9, 93
  land under Settled Land Acts, 83–4
  see Co-owners
Party-wall, 73–4
Patent, joint owners of, 57, 89–90
Payment into Court, in respect of expulsion, 73
Per my et per tout, 33, 56
Person, man and wife one, 6, 13, 17
Persona, of corporation, 2, 66, 98–100
  man and wife, 8, 9
  ancestor, 18
  parceners, 23
  joint tenants, 35
  tenants in common, 50
  partners, 66, 67, 68, 110
  parson, 100, 106
  king and crown, 106–8
  colonies, 107–8
  trade union, 109–110
Persona ficta, moralis, etc., 23, 99
Personae designatae, 25
Personality, *see Persona*
Personalty, tenancy by entireties applies to, 37
  parcenary does not apply to, 37
  rights and remedies of co-owners *inter se* in respect of, 90–7
Per tout et non per my, 11, 33
Pledge, joint, who may redeem, 57, 94–5
Ploughing ancient meadow, 76
Possession, unity of, 31, 33–4, 49, 71
Possession of one joint owner possession of all, 24, 34, 54
Possibility upon a possibility, 37
Prescription, tenants in common by, 50, 51
Presentation, *see* Advowson
Primogeniture, 18, 19, 20
  among women, 22
Privity of joint tenants, 31
  of tenants in common, 49
Profits, accounting for, under 4 Anne, 78–80
  mesne, *see* Mesne Profits
Purchase, joint in equal shares, 40

Rationabilis pars, 24, 46, 52, 71
Real and personal actions, 54–6
Real Property Limitation Act, 24, 26, 34, 54
Realty, rights and remedies of co-owners *inter se* in respect of, 71–84

Receipt, in joint mortgage, 40–1
Receiver, appointment of, 74–6
  under Judicature Act, 90–1
Redemption, suit by tenants in
    common, 56–7
  right of, on co-owners' pledge, 57,
    91–5
  one co-owner may secure whole
    equity of, 83
Registration, incorporation by, 3
Remainders, cross, 53–4
Remedies of co-owners *inter se*, 69–97
  see Co-owners
Rent, one joint tenant may distrain
    on another for, 45
  distress for, paid to one co-owner,
    74–5
  see Occupation rent
Rent-charge, *jus accrescendi* defeats,
    37–8
Repairs, allowance for, 80–1
Rights of co-owners *inter se*, 69–97
  see Co-owners
Roman law, rights of co-owners *inter
    se* at, 69
Rules of Supreme Court, as to parties,
    35, 67

Sale and partition, 26, 47–8, 53
  of ship, 88
Sale by Court, 47–8
Sale by one joint owner, effect of, 93–5
Scotland, descent of wife's share in, 6
  communio bonorum in, 10
  kingdom of, indivisible, 28
  partnership in, 67
Separate estate of married woman,
    13, 15–17, 43
Sergeanties, whether divisible, 27
Settled Land Acts, 83–4
Sever, intention to, in joint tenancy,
    39
Severance, of joint tenancy, 42–4
  see Partition
Sheriff, and common law partition, 26
Ships, co-owners of, 84–9, 93
Socage, estate in, impartible, 46
Societas, of husband and wife, 6
Société en commandite, 67–8
Soil, removal of, 73
Sone to the plough (or lowe), 21
Sovereign, as joint tenant, 31
  right to alien's moiety, 32
State, hostile to voluntary associa-
    tions, 2
Statutes,
  Action of Account (4 Anne), 13, 73,
    78–80
  Anonymous Partnership Act, 67
  Bodies Corporate Act, 1899, 32, 52
  Companies Act, 1862, 2, 3, 64, 67–8
  Conveyancing Act, 1881, 41, 50

Statutes,
  Copyhold Act, 1841, 47
  Frauds, Statute of, 25
  Gavelkind, 21
  Inclosure Act, 1895, 50
  Inclosure Acts, 26, 48
  Inheritance Act, 1833, 23
  Judicature Acts, 64, 66, 90–1
  Land Transfer Act, 1897, 18
  Larceny Act, 1868, 64
  Limited Partnerships Act, 68
  Married Women's Property Act,
    1882, 13, 15–17, 43
  Naturalisation Act, 1870, 32
  Partition (31 Hen. VIII. c. 1), 46,
    52–3
  Partition Acts, 26, 47, 53, 62
  Partnership Act, 1890, 62, 63
  Real Property Limitation Act, 1833,
    24, 26, 34, 54
  Settled Land Act, 1882, 83
  Settled Land Act, 1884, 84
  Settled Land Acts, 48
  Statute of Frauds, 25
  Statute of Tenures, 26
  Statute of Uses, 33, 51
  Tenures, Statute of, 26
  Trade Union Act, 1871, 109
  Trustee Acts, 24, 30
  Uses, Statute of, 33, 51
Stobbe, theories of man and wife, 7–11
Strassburg, ownership by man and
    wife in, 5
Subject and king, joint tenants, 31–2
Survivorship, right of, in tenancy by
    entireties, 11
  parcenary, 24
  joint tenancy, 35–8
    defeats devise, 37
    defeats charges, 37
    and agreement to alienate, 37, 43
    mischief of, 38–9
    and executory trusts, 40
  exceptions to, 38–42
    mortgages, 40–1
    joint traders, 41–2, 59–61
  and tenancy in common, 49–50
  in copyright, 37
  in title-deeds, 72

Tanistry, in Ireland, 21
Taunton Dean, borough-english in, 19
Tenancy by entireties, 11–17
  nature and origin of, 11
  founded on marriage, 13
  effect of gift to man and wife and
    third person, 13–16
  effect of divorce, 13
  effect of Married Women's Pro-
    perty Act on, 15, 16–17
  disappearing, 17
  see Tenants by Entireties

Tenancy in Common, 49–58
favoured by equity, 39–40, 51
origin of, 49, 51
unities in, 49
no survivorship, 49–50
dower and curtesy in, 50
how extinguished, 52
partition in, 52–3, 62
and cross remainders, 53–4
unlike partnership, 61–3
no agency or trusteeship in, 61–2, 78
no lien in, 62
see Tenants in Common
Tenancy, Joint, *see* Joint Tenancy
Tenant for life, co-owners constituting the, 83–4
Tenants by Entireties, 11–17
joint tenants becoming, 13
becoming joint tenants, 13
effect of divorce, 13
effect of unity of man and wife, 13–17
and personalty, 37
rights of, *inter se*, 70
Tenants in common, 49–58
joint tenants becoming, 42–3, 45, 51
not one person in law, 50
have several estate, 50
making joint lease, 50
leasing to one another, 51
partition by, 52–3
possession of one and of all, 54
suing jointly, 54
suing severally, 55–6
mortgage by, 56–7
pledge by, 57, 94–5
of patent, 57, 89–90
of trademark, 57, 89–90
of copyright, 57–8, 89–90
whether partners are, 61–2, 63–4
of mine, 76–7, 80
may also be partners, 76
of ships, 79, 84–9
under Settled Land Acts, 83–4
rights and remedies *inter se, see* Co-owners
Tenants, Joint, *see* Joint Tenants
Tenures, Statute of, 26
Timber, cutting of, 75, 76
Time, unity of, 32–3, 49
Title, unity of, 31, 32, 49
Title-deeds, right to, 71–2
Titles of honour, indivisible, 27
Towns, ownership by, 99, 101–106

Trademark, part-owners of, 57, 89–90
Traders, no *jus accrescendi* amongst, 41, 59
see Merchants, Law Merchant
Trade union, as co-owning group, 103
as unit, 109–10
Trade Union Act, 1871, 109
Trespass, 73, 86, 91–3
injunction against, 90–1
Trover, 57, 91–3
Trust, co-ownership by, 3, 103
disclosure of in mortgage deed, 41
Trustee Acts, 24, 30
Trustees, joint tenants, 30, 36
Trusteeship, in partnership, 61, 63
none in other co-ownerships, 69–70

United Hand, group of the, 9
Uses, Statute of, 33, 51

Valuation, compulsory sale at a, 48
Village Community, 100
co-ownership by, 100–106
Voluntary association, State and right of, 2

Warren, partition of, 27
Waste, pleadings in action to prevent, 35
injunction against, 76, 90–1
Whale, rights of co-owners of a, 92
Wife, husband and, *see* Man and wife
jewels of, 5
power to make will, 5
could not steal from husband, 6, 13
effect of Married Women's Property Act, 13, 15–17
criminal liability of, 17
Will, of joint tenant, *jus accrescendi* and, 37, 44
joint tenancy created by, 30, 51
Wills, mutual by joint tenants, 44
Writ, *de partitione facienda*, 26, 46, 52
de rationabili parte, 71
ejectione firmae, 72
Mortdauncestor, 71
Nuper obiit, 71
of contribution, 71, 82
Wrong, joint tenants acquiring by, 30
Würtemberg, ownership by man and wife in, 4